A

SHORT INTRODUCTION

TO THE

ANCIENT GREEK

THEATER

A

SHORT INTRODUCTION

TO THE

ANCIENT
GREEK
THEATER

Graham Ley

THE UNIVERSITY OF CHICAGO PRESS

CHICAGO & LONDON

The University of Chicago Press, Chicago 60637
The University of Chicago Press, Ltd., London

© 1991 by The University of Chicago
All rights reserved. Published 1991
Printed in the United States of America

00 99 98 97 96 95 94 93 92 91 5 4 3 2 1

Library of Congress Cataloging-in-Publication Data

Ley, Graham.
A short introduction to the Ancient Greek theater / Graham Ley.
        p.   cm.
Includes bibliographical references and index.
ISBN 0-226-47759-2 (cloth). — ISBN 0-226-47760-6 (pbk.)
1. Theater—Greece—History. 2. Greek drama—History and
criticism. I. Title.
PA3201/L47   1991
792′.0938—dc20   91-11115
                                                                CIP

GRAHAM LEY has taught theater studies and Greek drama at the University
of London and the University of Auckland, New Zealand. He has adapted
Greek plays for sound and stage, and directed for the theater.

CONTENTS

LIST OF PLANS AND ILLUSTRATIONS

PLANS

.

PLATES
(following page 87)

PREFACE

I SHOULD like to express my thanks to all those who have helped in the formation of this volume. Students from the Universities of London and Auckland are foremost in the list, but I should like to include Michael Ewans, Meg and Marcus Wilson, Philip Hardie, Stig Rudberg, John Penwill, Tony Boyle, and Teresa Rodrigues, and to thank Richard Mazillius for drawing the diagrams. Richard Hamilton of Bryn Mawr provided many acute comments in his reading for the University of Chicago Press, and I am extremely grateful for his time and attention. Firm acknowledgment is also due to the associate director of the Press, Penelope Kaiserlian, for her careful guidance through to publication, and perhaps especially to David Grene, coeditor of *The Complete Greek Tragedies,* for his advice and support throughout. The edited text has benefited from the amendments suggested by Jo Ann Kiser for the Press; any flaws that remain are my own. I should like to dedicate the book to my family.

Author's Note: Those exact line references I have given are to the Greek of the Oxford Classical Text of Aeschylus, Sophocles, Euripides, and Aristophanes. Most modern translations provide some indications of line numbers, but unfortunately these vary considerably in their frequency.

ACKNOWLEDGMENTS

I AM GRATEFUL to David Rudkin and Margaret Ramsay Ltd. for permission to quote from the Foreword to David Rudkin's version of Euripides' *Hippolytus*, published by Heinemann Educational Books in 1980. The translation of the choral song from Euripides' *Hippolytus* is from the version of that play by David Grene in *The Complete Greek Tragedies*, published by the University of Chicago Press, and I should like to thank David Grene and the Press for allowing its inclusion.

The illustrations are reproduced by kind permission from Antikenmuseum Basel und Sammlung Ludwig (plate 1); H. L. Pierce Fund, courtesy Museum of Fine Arts, Boston (plate 2); Ashmolean Museum, Oxford (plate 3); J. Paul Getty Museum, Malibu (plate 4); Staatliche Museen zu Berlin, Antikensammlung (plate 5); Antikenmuseum Berlin, Staatliche Museen, preussischer Kulturbesitz (plate 6). My thanks are due to the staff in the photographic and publications departments of all these museums for their help.

The short comment by J. P. Sartre on adaptation is from the introduction to his adaptation of Euripides' *Trojan Women*, English version by Ronald Duncan, published by Hamish Hamilton in 1967. The selection of short extracts from versions of Aeschylus' *Agamemnon* is taken, in the order of their presentation in the text below, from: Robert Potter's eighteenth-century translation; *The Agamemnon*, translated into English rhyming verse by Gilbert Murray, London, George Allen and Unwin, 1920; *The Agamemnon of Aeschylus*, translated by Louis MacNeice, London, Faber and Faber, 1936; *The Complete Greek Tragedies*, edited by David Grene and Richmond Lattimore, *Aeschylus 1, Oresteia*, translated with an introduction by Richmond Lattimore, Chicago, the University of Chicago Press, 1953; *Agamemnon,* edited with a commentary by Eduard Fraenkel, *Volume 1, Prolegomena. Text. Translation,* Oxford, Oxford University Press, 1950; Robert Lowell, *The Oresteia of Aeschylus,* New York, Farrar, Strauss, Giroux, 1978; *The Oresteia,* translated by Robert Fagles, Harmondsworth, Penguin Books, 1977; Tony Harrison, *Dramatic Verse 1973–1985,* Newcastle upon Tyne, Bloodaxe Books, 1985.

The drawings are by Richard Mazillius, to designs by the author.

A
SHORT INTRODUCTION
TO THE
ANCIENT GREEK
THEATER

INTRODUCTION

THE TEXTS of ancient Greek tragedy and comedy have survived for over two thousand years, because small numbers of people thought they were worth preserving. Most modern readers meet them in translation, and the readership for these translations is perhaps a larger one than the plays have had at any other stage in their life. So it seems right that, for the reader of what was originally a performed work, some attempt should be made to indicate the original performance conditions.

Readers in translation are obviously dependent on those who have learned the ancient language; and it is fair to say that knowledge of the original language is at least a safeguard, if not essential, for the task of reconstruction that faces the professional historian of theater. But probably more significant than that is a wide reading of the plays, preferably over a number of years.

The main reason for this, perhaps ironically, is that the plays themselves actually provide the most detailed body of evidence on the theatrical conditions for which they were designed. I mention irony because for many of the original audience nothing could have seemed more self-evident than the shape of the playing space, the color and design of the costumes, and the styles of performance presented to them.

The position for us, of course, is completely reversed. With the exceptions of archaeological evidence, some vase painting, and occasional comment or anecdote, the material form of ancient theater is substantially lost. What is left is a task of reconstruction, largely based on deduction from the "scripts" that survive, with alternatives weighed, and one chosen. There can be no guarantee that any reconstruction will finally be accurate; but it should be consistent, and provide at least a coherent vision of what for the original audience must have been one particular arrangement at any one time.

The reason we can speak with some confidence of "one particular arrangement" is that most of the ancient Greek texts we have, with possibly one or two exceptions, were written for first performance in one place, and in one theater. The writers of the surviving ancient Greek tragedies and comedies were all Athenians; and the dramatic festivals for which they composed, in a period that stretches effectively from 475 to 400 B.C., took place in the theater dedicated to the god Dionysus, on the southern slope of the *akropolis,* the citadel of Athens (fig. 1). In general it is clear from the surviving plays, to some of which specific dates are attached, that the conditions of performance varied very little over this period, as might be expected when a single theater is the prime location for all major theatrical activity.

I have tried to concentrate in this short book largely on questions affecting presentation, and on what we might term the "theatrical apparatus": the material resources of theater that any prospective writer aims to deploy. There are many other books of many different kinds on the Greek theater, and on Greek drama, and the reader is advised to consult those in answer to any question which this one fails to satisfy. As some help in this respect I have appended a short bibliography of works in English which might be next in line for someone with strong interests in this area.

For visual illustration, I have included a number of photographs of vase paintings from the period, and several schematic diagrams to provide some indication of the nature of the performance space and its place in the city of Athens. References are made to further illustrations from works cited in the concluding bibliography. (The titles in the references are abbreviated. See the bibliography for list of abbreviations.) The forms of the names of the tragic playwrights, and of their plays and

fig.1   relative location of theater, assembly
          and *agora* in Athens

the characters in them, are those used in *The Complete Greek Tragedies,* published by the University of Chicago Press. Some other names are given their familiar spellings. Less familiar Greek names, and the terms collected in the glossary at the back of this book, are transliterated (using "ch" in place of "kh": so *choros,* not *khoros*).

4

One final note: I have not attempted to include Menander, an Athenian comic writer who composed approximately in the years 320–290 B.C., because of the length of time that separates him from the period embracing the work of the other playwrights, and because a study of his theatrical practice for that reason needs to be made independently. So this work concentrates on what is known as the fifth century, 500–400 B.C., and plays presented at that time in the theater of Dionysus at Athens.

◉

GREEK DRAMA

GREEK DRAMA, as usually described, includes the surviving tragedies (and satyr plays) of Aeschylus (c. 525–456 B.C.), Sophocles (c. 496–406 B.C.), and Euripides (c. 485–406 B.C.), and the comedies of Aristophanes (c. 450–385 B.C.) and Menander (c. 342–290 B.C.). Of these writers, Aeschylus is clearly the earliest, Sophocles and Euripides are near contemporaries, and Aristophanes is the youngest in the fifth century, though his writing career overlaps those of Sophocles and Euripides. Menander belongs to the end of the following century, and wrote comedies of a noticeably different kind from those of Aristophanes.

Since these plays are the primary source of interest in the Greek theater, as well as the most substantial evidence for its nature, some further details are necessary.

There are three kinds of play mentioned above. Of these, tragedy was considered predominantly serious and comedy was humorous. Satyr plays were composed by the tragedians, and were a grotesque relief from tragedy. It seems to be the case that no tragic writer wrote comedies, or comic writer tragedies.

Tragedy took its subject matter largely from the *muthoi* (myths or stories) which were expressed in the older narrative epic poems, of which only two, the *Iliad* and the *Odyssey* ascribed to Homer, survive. Comedy, in the hands of Aristophanes, was usually a contemporary fantasy, and was intended to be directly funny, as well as crude. The satyr play takes its name from the curious half-human, half-bestial creatures who were inevitable participants in the action, and who were called satyrs (plate 3). It has nothing to do with the later Roman form of poetry called "satire."

It is useful to speak of "surviving" plays because each writer, comic or tragic, composed far more than the number passed down from antiquity to the modern period. In the case of the later writer Menander, whose work was extremely popular in Egypt under its Greek and Roman administrations, excavations and careful methods of examining archaeological finds have revealed large fragments of his comedies. For the earlier dramatists, a modern reader is still mostly dependent on those few scripts that were copied in manuscript and preserved until the art of printing made them more widely available. A list of these surviving plays is given at the back of this book, with an approximate chronology. The gaps are very large: Aeschylus composed about eighty plays, Sophocles about one hundred and twenty, Euripides perhaps about ninety, and Aristophanes at least forty. In addition to these writers there were many more, some known by name, whose works are mostly lost, though some fragments remain, as do some fragments from the major playwrights.

◻

THE ORGANIZATION OF
THE FESTIVALS

6

THE FESTIVALS of Dionysus at Athens which included dramatic performances were known as the City, or Great, Dionysia and the Lenaea. The first of these was instituted before the beginning of the fifth century; dramatic performances at the Lenaea were officially recognized much later, just before 440 B.C. The City Dionysia remained by far the more important of the two dramatic festivals, though a comic writer such as Aristophanes seems to have written quite readily for both. The Lenaea took place in January, and the City Dionysia in late March/April. The likelihood is that almost all the surviving plays, both comedies and tragedies, were originally composed for performance in the theater of Dionysus, though there may be one or two exceptions.

The god Dionysus was one of the Olympian deities honored at Athens and widely elsewhere in the Greek world. In origin an ecstatic god, he was celebrated in a song known as the dithyramb, and his followers in myth were satyrs, lecherous and drunken, and *mainades,* the "mad women" of his rites. The association of drama with his festivals seems to be connected with an emphasis on song and dance in his worship, as well as on the mask. The City Dionysia was probably developed well before the end of the preceding century, but the details as we have them are of its organization under the democracy.

A tragic writer normally wrote three tragedies and one satyr play for one presentation at the City Dionysia. If the tragedies were connected in theme, then the presentation of those three plays is now known as a trilogy. Comic writers presented only one play at a time, though they might, it seems, write for both festivals in the same year. Performances at the Lenaea and the City Dionysia were competitions in honor of the patron god.

At the City Dionysia each year three tragic writers competed against each other, and either three or five comic writers. There was no competition between comedies and tragedies. The audience must have watched four or five plays a day, for three or four days.

Apart from the major city festivals, there were also local celebrations in honor of Dionysus, held usually in the middle of winter in the townships of Attica, the region of which Athens was the capital city. There is clear evidence for the performance of plays at a number of these country Dionysia in the fourth century, and it is quite possible that some of these productions originated in the fifth century, certainly in locations like the Piraeus, the port of Athens. Whether the plays on these occasions were new, or revivals of popular tragedies and comedies seen at the major festivals, is not altogether clear. But later evidence suggests revivals, and the writers whose work survives seem to have concentrated on presenting new plays at the city festivals, notably the City Dionysia.

The official primarily responsible for the organization of the City Dionysia was the *archon*, a magistrate chosen annually by lot, and by whose name the year was known. It was to this magistrate, who assumed office in midsummer, that prospective playwrights "applied for a chorus," namely for official acceptance as one of the three tragedians, or three or five comic writers, whose works were to be performed in the following spring. By what criterion the decision was made is unknown, nor is it clear how the playwrights presented their case to the magistrate.

The further organization of tragic, satyric, and comic production, and the bulk of the expense, then devolved on wealthy private citizens, selected as *choregoi*, or producers, for each playwright. The state paid for the actors, and the *choregos* paid for the training and costume of the chorus. There would appear to be a gap of about six months or more between the selection of a playwright and the performance of his work, and

by at least the end of the fifth century there was a public an-
nouncement of the subjects of the plays, the *proagon*, shortly
before the period of performance.

The introduction of a public subsidy for poorer citizens to
attend the performances is attributed to the Athenian politi-
cian Pericles (d. 429 B.C.), and it is likely that tickets would
have been in use from this period forward in the fifth century.

◻

THE WRITER

THE OFFICIAL TERM for the playwright in the festival records
is *didaskalos,* which means "teacher" or "trainer," and this title
refers to an original function as trainer of the chorus, a group
of dancing singers who formed the core of dramatic performance. But later, with the introduction of solo actors, the term
will probably have been understood to cover the preparation
of a fixed script and musical form for production. It seems that
the playwright was also regularly responsible for what we
would now call theatrical direction, as well as for the composition of spoken and sung text. But the comic writer Aristophanes handed over some of his plays to other directors, and scat-
tered evidence suggests this practice may not have been
uncommon for comedy in the later fifth century. The degree to
which an enthusiastic and committed *choregos,* by taking care
of much of the expense of the production, might intrude upon
direction is unclear; but it would seem that his principal responsibility was for the fitness, skills, and presentation of the
chorus.

All plays were composed in verse. The spoken verse, largely
for the actors, was usually in the iambic meter, considered close
to the rhythms of normal speech. Songs for the chorus, and
occasionally for actors, were in a variety of meters and modes.

One essential for the playwright would almost certainly be an advanced training in the art of (choral) song composition, and probably in dance. All the dramatic writers whom we know seem to have started composing plays as young men, which suggests that the activity followed closely on education, which will have involved some attention to the work of prominent past poets and songwriters.

Choice of form may have been easy, because it was definite. For the intending tragic writer, there was a brief period in the earlier fifth century when it was possible to compose on events taken from recent military struggles. This was apparently succeeded by an almost constant expectation that subjects for tragedies would be taken from the lives and actions of mythical figures, as these were represented by the poems that existed about them, or by the spoken traditions or rituals associated with them and with various localities. These sources—when combined with the curious cowardice and licentiousness that characterized the unvarying chorus of satyrs—would also provide much of the substance for the composition of satyr plays.

For the comic writer, there is the evidence of Aristophanes, who would seem to be as attracted to the opportunity to make his audience laugh at the fantastic aspirations of his characters as he is to the chance to be amusingly provocative on issues of contemporary concern. A similar, if not the same, capacity for the composition of spoken verse and song as in tragedy and a fascination with the techniques of theatrical humor would provide the backbone of the art. For later comedy, in the work of Menander, there is evidence for a greater ethical interest in the actions and motives of comic characters, which may reflect the influence of contemporary philosophy. Both comic writers show a profound interest in tragedy.

Although successful playwrights were granted a prize, it is not known what this amounted to, nor is it likely that the existence of a prize encouraged the development of a class of playwrights who supported themselves by composition. The evidence is to the contrary, and the surviving writers appear to have belonged to the wide category of Athenians whose landholding was large enough to support them, and to provide them with the leisure to involve themselves in public life.

Biographical details on the writers are not substantial, and where they do exist it is not clear how much reliance should be placed on them. But tradition records that Sophocles was prominent in music and dance from an early age, and that he originally performed as an actor in his own early plays. His later role in public life included service as a general, and as treasurer for the Athenian military alliance. His respect for organized religion is also recorded, as are the statements that he wrote a work on the chorus (now lost) and founded a religious association in honor of the Muses. His son, Iophon, became a playwright, and Sophocles himself is said never to have been placed third in a dramatic competition. It is a reasonably convincing picture, and may well be accurate.

◧

THE THEATER

THE LOCATION for the City festival of Dionysus was the theater in the precinct of the god on the south slope of the citadel of Athens, the *akropolis*. Many changes were made to the theater in antiquity, and the present ruins largely reflect the foundations and first levels of a version of the theater constructed far later than the fifth century B.C.

Archaeology considers layers, and investigations of the ruins of the theater of Dionysus, along with comparisons with other Greek theaters, have established some reasonable conclusions about the nature of the original playing space and its development.

The earliest evidence for performances in the precinct seems to be for a circular dancing space, an *orchestra,* on a flattened terrace at the foot of the hill, and associated with a small temple of Dionysus (figs. 2a and 2b). This suggests the presence of choral songs and dances. The choice of the slope of the *akropolis* for the *orchestra,* and perhaps in principle for the precinct of Dionysus, may well have been dependent on the ease with which a hillside can accommodate an audience. This would then provide a natural *theatron,* or "watching-place." Other evidence suggests, contrastingly, that some early performances may have taken place in the *agora,* on ground set aside in the city for trade and cult (fig. 1), and in which there was still an area known as the *orchestra* at the end of the fifth century. But by the time of the earliest surviving plays there can be little doubt that dramatic performances took place in the theater.

The developed shape of the theater (the term comes to be applied to the whole) includes three components (figs. 3a and 3b): an extensive *theatron,* with the hill hollowed out and stepped, perhaps mostly with boards, but later consolidated in stone, accommodating eventually up to fourteen thousand spectators; an *orchestra,* probably circular in the fifth century, in which a chorus could sing and dance; and, additionally, the *skene* or scene building, which included a door. Of these three components, the *skene* poses the most problems, because the foundations provide no precise evidence for its elevation, and there are no certain illustrations of a *skene* dating from the fifth century.

The earliest surviving plays—the earlier tragedies of Aeschylus—seem to have been performed without a scene building. But the surviving trilogy known as the *Oresteia,* produced in 458 B.C., initiates a period, which then lasts as long as the convention itself, in which a scene building of some sort is clearly involved in the performance both of tragedies and comedies.

The word *skene* simply means tent, and presumably this re-

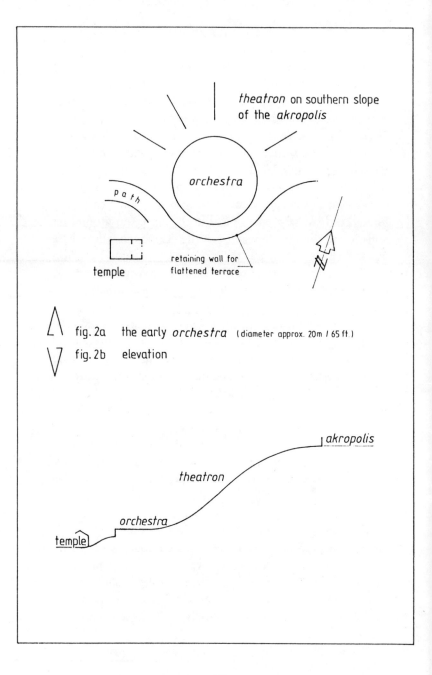

theatron on southern slope
of the akropolis

orchestra

path

temple

retaining wall for
flattened terrace

fig. 2a   the early orchestra (diameter approx. 20m / 65 ft.)

fig. 2b   elevation

akropolis

theatron

orchestra

temple

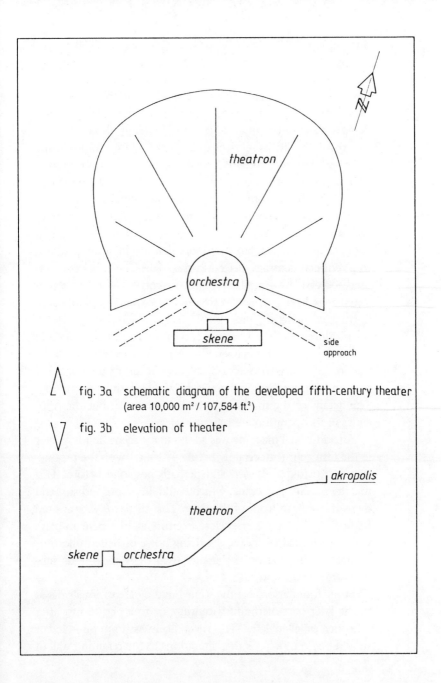

fig. 3a   schematic diagram of the developed fifth-century theater
           (area 10,000 m² / 107,584 ft.²)

fig. 3b   elevation of theater

flects a time when a tent was used. But in the first play of the *Oresteia* a character appears on the roof, and in the earlier plays of Aeschylus it is difficult to find any suggestion that a tent was deployed as a substantial indication of setting, though the actors certainly did have to change masks and costume during their performance. Perhaps a *skene* was used for this purpose.

14

The initial construction of a solid *skene* would almost certainly have been from wood. From the beginning there are clear signs that it contained the machinery later known as an *ekkuklema,* which appears to have been a mobile platform that could be projected from the doors that are logically assumed to have been centrally placed in the *skene*. The *ekkuklema* was used for display—regularly of recent corpses—and if it projected it is likely to have rested when forward on some supporting substructure, presumably also of wood. By the time of the production of the *Oresteia,* and of the known construction of the *skene,* the Athenians had considerable experience in the traction of heavy wooden objects, as a result of the construction and renovation of their many fighting ships (triremes). The details of the machinery remain unknown, but the principles of its operation are relatively clear.

An additional machine was added to the scene building later in the fifth century, certainly before 431 B.C., with the production of Euripides' *Medea,* and perhaps not long before. This was the *mechane,* or crane, which could lift actors and suspend them above or in front of the *skene*. That the *mechane* was used for striking visual effect is clear from its involvement in plays where an animal (Pegasus, the flying horse of Bellerophon) or an object (the chariot of the sun, used by Medea) adds substance to the illusion.

Stone foundations for the scene building are variously dated to the later part of the fifth century, or to a period just after 400 B.C. or even later. The most likely assumption—and it should be no more—is that alterations to the retaining wall of the *theatron,* known to be made in the time of Pericles in connection with the construction of the neighboring Odeum, should be associated with developments toward permanence in the *skene,* which could then accommodate the *mechane.* Further stages in adaptation and construction finally resulted in both *theatron* and *skene* being fully established in expensive stone by the later part of the fourth century.

15

The major problems concerning the construction and form of the *skene* are accompanied by some doubts over the shape of the *orchestra,* of which the regular circle familiar from pictures of the later theater at Epidaurus may prove to be an inaccurate representation. So the diagrams presented here must be taken to be no more than provisional, in sketching the relation of parts to the whole.

□

SCENOGRAPHY

SKENOGRAPHIA, literally "painting of/on a *skene,*" with an associated term *skiagraphia,* which refers to the "painting of shadows," are the words used to describe what on occasions has been doubted, namely the indication of theatrical setting by painting, most probably on panels. This innovation is ascribed either to Aeschylus or to Sophocles in the sources, and these indications, if reliable, would place it in the same immediate period as the introduction of the third actor ("Actors," below) and the construction of the *skene.*

Major narrative painting in Athens and elsewhere in Greece was displayed on the interior walls of public buildings, and seems to date as a distinct development from the period of the earliest surviving plays. This is clearly interesting in relation to the construction of the *skene,* because the later foundations provide evidence for a facade, in a series of postholes on either side of what must be a foundation for a central door, and a facade could easily be used to display a series of painted panels indicating setting.

The Roman writer Vitruvius states in his treatise on architecture that the painter Agatharchos, who worked for Aeschylus and left a commentary on his creation, influenced other near-contemporaries to write on the use of perspective in scene painting. Vitruvius explicitly refers to the use of perspective in the representation of buildings, and temples and grander private houses, or "palaces," were certainly two of the most regular settings for tragedy. It would not be difficult to match this consistency in "background" with Vitruvius' statement, and with a growing interest in a limited form of perspective, stimulated by the opportunity to decorate and define the theatrical *skene*.

Further evidence concerns the satyr plays, which would appear to have made repeated use of a cave for their settings. This same, or a similar, location appears also in surviving tragedy (Sophocles' *Philoctetes*) and in comedy (Aristophanes' *Birds*), and evidence from vase painting (plates 5 and 6, Euripides' lost tragedies *Andromeda* and *Antiope*) confirms that rocks, trees, and shrubs were associated with representations of the cave in tragedy.

A striking change of setting in one tragedy (Sophocles' *Ajax,* from military tent to deserted shoreline), and the contrasting locations of plays linked in one presentation (Euripides' *Helen,* set in front of a palace, and his lost *Andromeda,* set on the seacoast in front of a cave) might best be explained by reference to the resources of painting on panels. The limited range for visual representation would then contain the temple, the palace or larger private house, the cave or other natural setting, and an occasional ironic variation, such as the farmer's hut in Euripides' *Electra*.

It cannot be at all clear, from the nature of the available

Comic

evidence, whether *skenographia* was considered by later theorists to have been used for comic performance in this period. But the surviving scripts can certainly remove performers and a diversity of properties abruptly ("The Playing Space" and "Distance and Physical Action" below), and abruptness in the change of setting in some surviving plays might reflect the same unrecorded activity in support of presentation. If the satyr play made use of a cave, then *skenographia* should not be excluded as a possibility for a form of performance as strongly visual as fifth-century comedy.

17

▣

MASKS, COSTUME, AND PROPERTIES

MASKS (*PROSOPA*) and decorated costume are known to have been significant elements of the worship of the god Dionysus at Athens, and it is at least likely that their use in rites and celebration predates the emergence of drama. Specifically, vase paintings in nondramatic contexts show a mask of the god suspended from a tree with a decorated robe hanging below it to form an icon of the deity, around which dancers may be gathered. The existence of these material elements would allow, with little immediate innovation, for the presentation of early drama.

Illustrations of theatrical masks on Athenian vases from the fifth century reveal a full head mask, with no particular distortion, for tragic performance: of a kind that appears to take its dimensions from the contradictory demands of close assimilation to the distance between the performers' eyes and mouth (laterally and vertically) and the need to envelop the head (*DFA,* figs. 32 and 33). The result is, almost inevitably, an exaggerated jaw. Chorus members for tragedy were masked and costumed in a very similar manner to actors, as more than one vase from the period shows (plate 2). The materials used were fragile, and almost certainly light: linen and wood are possible components, and some form of paste (plaster, mortar) seems a far more plausible candidate for the shaping and stiffening of the facial areas than the only likely alternative, wax. Masks may have been stored, but the differentiation needed in the range of roles or the requirements of actors will have meant that the mask makers, the *prosopopoioi,* will have been fairly active. For the City Dionysia in one year alone, fifteen to seventeen plays with an average of twenty and more performers add up to a formidable total.

More can be said about masks than is probably appropriate here. Some of the major points are these:

For comedy, there is strong evidence that some masks were modeled directly on life, to provide a caricature of a known individual. Some politicians, playwrights, and other figures, notably the philosopher Socrates, were perhaps portrayed in this way.

Comic masks were distortions, but unfortunately almost all the visual evidence applies to periods later than the fifth century (but see plate 4). A rigid categorization by type, and perhaps by masks in an extended but fixed series (e.g., the running slave, the old man, the young girl, etc.), is almost certainly a later development, though it may well have its roots in Aristophanic comedy.

The scripts on a number of occasions reveal some characteristics of a particular mask. One of the best examples is the picture that emerges of the mask of the god Dionysus when he is apprehended and questioned by Pentheus in Euripides' tragedy *The Bacchae.*

The use of masks lent itself to specific effects. Not only did it mean that an individual actor might appear and reappear as several different characters, but a powerful effect might

be achieved by altering or changing the mask for the same
character within a play. In Euripides' *Helen* Helen enters
the scene building to reappear with a change of costume
and an altered mask, in pretended mourning; and in Sophocles' *Oedipus the King* and Euripides' *Hecuba* both Oedipus and Polymestor enter the scene building toward the
climax of the plays to reappear blinded.

Euripides may well have made use of the same mask for
Helen in his *Trojan Women* in 415 B.C. as for his radically
different presentation of Helen in the play of that name
dated securely at 412 B.C. Other possibilities of reuse may
also be found from the same period, in Euripides' surviving tragedies.

The costume for tragedy was, it appears, always decorative,
though it seems to have been based largely on a selective presentation of familiar, contemporary garments. There is some
evidence, from vase paintings, that theatrical costume became
more elaborate during the course of the century (compare
plates 1 and 2 with plate 5), and further evidence confirms that
oriental or non-Greek costume was distinctive (*IGD* III.2.1).
Fabric might also be used as a substantial property, as it is in
the reception of Agamemnon into the scene building in the
Oresteia of Aeschylus. The weaving or dyeing of elaborate garments is attested for various forms of cult, and the adaptation
of this attention to theatrical performance cannot have posed
many serious problems. At least in tragedy performers might
be given soft calf-length boots, perhaps known as *kothornoi*,
with a curved toe and slipper base suitable for swift movement
(plate 2).

Costume is of crucial importance in determining characters
or chorus by status, sex, provenance, or condition of life. In
his comedy *Frogs*, Aristophanes suggests that Aeschylus had
used more solemn costume than the rags favored by Euripides.
But in the earliest surviving play of Aeschylus, *The Persians*, the

19

defeated Persian king Xerxes returns in tatters; while in Euripides' *Andromache* and *Trojan Women* Hermione and Helen appear in finery, in explicit contrast to women who are slaves. Slaves, refugees, non-Greeks, warriors, powerful men and women, gods, and the servants of gods all make their appearance in the surviving tragedies of Aeschylus, and there is little to suggest that this range was narrowed over the course of the century. Some varieties of garment may be illustrated accurately on the available vases; but again it is Euripides' *Bacchae*, with its ironic delight in dressing the rigid authoritarian ruler Pentheus in the clothing of a woman worshipper of Dionysus, which provides the most exact and detailed description of any one costume in the surviving tragedies.

For comedy, there is occasional evidence that the actors might wear a hugely exaggerated penis, as part of a traditional costume dependent on the close association of the male member (*phallos*) with the worship of the god Dionysus (plate 4). Otherwise, costume design might vary wildly, and fantastically, with the concept of the play: in Aristophanes' *Birds* there are clear indications that each chorus member represented a different wild bird, and the predominance of animal choruses in fifth-century comedy (*Wasps, Frogs*) and of inanimate objects (*Clouds* and *Transport Ships*, the latter a lost play) suggests visual ingenuity on an elaborate scale. An immense variety of comic costume, combined in spectacle, is also apparent from the opening scene of Aristophanes' *Acharnians*.

For the satyr play, we have the benefit of a representation of a complete cast on what seems to be a celebration vase, from about the end of the century (*DFA,* fig. 49; *HGRT,* fig. 20). From this painting, and from others, it is clear that the satyr mask was snub-nosed, and that a loincloth of linen or of goatskin was worn, with an erect but not exaggerated penis and a horsetail. The leader of the satyrs was known as Silenus, who would seem to have been characterized by a more complete body stocking covered in white fur, and portrayed as old and white-haired.

Properties are abundant in comedy, with a particular emphasis on all the equipment of an *oikos,* or household, with repeated attention to kitchen implements. Contrived properties may form a spectacular opening to a play, such as the giant dung beetle attached to the *mechane* in Aristophanes' *Peace,* or a visual adjunct to what is already a preposterous scene, such as the doubtlessly enlarged and possibly human-powered cheese grater in the remarkable trial of the dog in *Wasps.*

21

In this last case, a property may come close to being a costume, and for tragedy a more restrained use of props could confirm any expectation received from myth, or from familiar illustration in painting or sculpture. It is inherently likely that both Apollo and Artemis will carry a bow, and, possibly, threaten to use it. So, for all three forms of play in which he could be made to appear, the expectation will be that Heracles should be clothed in a lion skin and be seen carrying a club, with perhaps his bow slung over his shoulders.

Properties may be a means of identification, but that also may lead to a wider significance. Philoctetes, in Sophocles' play, is the inheritor of Heracles' bow; but it is fundamentally the bow, if not the man himself, that Odysseus and Neoptolemus have come to take with them to Troy, and its presence and its handling divides and unites the characters repeatedly throughout the tragedy.

Aristophanes parodies Euripides' use of properties (as well as costume) in his comedy *Acharnians,* and their significance in setting the tone of a play is paralleled by their crucial action within a play. A casket conveys the deadly robe to the daughter of Creon in Euripides' *Medea,* and another carries a similarly deadly robe to Heracles in Sophocles' *Women of Trachis.* Orestes stands to one side in Sophocles' *Electra* while his sister laments over an empty urn, supposedly containing his ashes.

Properties are of the essence of Athenian theater, and their great advantage for a modern vision of performance is that we can rely very often on decisive references to them in the scripts.

◙

CHORUS

THE GREEK WORD *choros* describes a group of people expected to sing and dance. The chorus for tragedy was apparently increased in number near the middle of the fifth century from twelve to fifteen; the chorus for comedy numbered twenty-four. There is no clear evidence for the size of the satyr chorus.

The history of the *choros* in Greek society is a long and complex one, and is bound up firmly with many varieties of Greek poetry, apart from drama. Most simply expressed, it is clear that songs or dances accompanied decisive events in the lives of Greek communities, and that eventually literacy, namely the record offered to us by the reintroduction of writing into Greece before 700 B.C., permits us to glimpse the organization of what originally may have been spontaneous or traditional forms into what we recognize as poetry. Those skilled in composition (verbal and musical) might be required or requested to provide a song for a particular event, such as a marriage, an athletic victory, the funeral of a member of a wealthy family, or a religious festival. This practice continued well into the fifth century and beyond, and many of the songs will have been sung by a chorus, often acting as representatives of a community.

A tragic *choros* in honor of the god Dionysus is first mentioned in connection with the sixth century, not at Athens; but convincing evidence for the widespread existence of *choroi* throughout the Greek world (in the western Greek settlements in Sicily and Italy, in Sparta, on the island of Delos in honor of the gods Apollo and Artemis) makes particular explanations for their presence at Athens unnecessary.

The use of the mask in Dionysiac worship may well have encouraged representation. The activities of *choroi* were in any case performances, and the presence of a composer as trainer (*didaskalos,* the later "playwright") is hardly surprising. What does seem to be distinct is the step by which this figure—and, for Athens, the earliest name is Thespis—began to take a part in the performance, from which origins the concept of the actor, and the speaking parts, gradually arose.

If tragedy was in origin "a" choral song, one of many different kinds but characterized by its dedication to Dionysus, then the major difference between that and the form that confronts us as developed "drama" is constituted by the juxtaposition of spoken sections and song. The role of the chorus in the surviving plays of Aeschylus is often substantial, with extensive sections of the play dependent on the continuity achieved through choral song and dance. In later tragedy the standard pattern is for this contribution to be made in a more distinctly intermittent way, as a series of independent "songs"—usually known as "odes," from the Greek word for song—which reveal a tendency toward the end of the century to discard their direct relevance to the action of the play.

For comedy, the situation is far more problematic, because the earliest surviving plays are very late (the earliest, Aristophanes' *Acharnians,* was produced in 425 B.C.), and because the origins and development of comedy as a theatrical form rapidly became obscure even in antiquity. One likely explanation sees the origin of comedy in a *komos,* a disorderly and irreverent procession in honor of the god Dionysus. The introduction of comedy into the City festival at a later date than tragedy, in 485 B.C., and the number granted to its chorus (double that originally given to tragedy) might then suggest that comedy, in its theatrical form, was in part modeled on the precedent given by tragedy.

Certain aspects of the comic chorus as it is found in the plays of Aristophanes appear to be traditional elements, though how far back these traditions go is impossible to judge. Of these the most notable is what was known as the *parabasis:* at a relatively central moment of the drama the chorus "steps forward/aside," its members perhaps disencumbering themselves of any properties they may have, and addresses the audience directly in an apparently corrective manner and on behalf of the dramatist.

The recurrence of an animal chorus for comedy has been mentioned. Here again, tradition is evident, because vase paintings from the early fifth century and before show men dressed as birds; men as horses, with other men riding on their backs (*IGD* I.9, *DTC* pl. VII: Aristophanes' *Knights* suggests a comparison); and men riding on dolphins and ostriches (*DTC* pl. VIII.b), in what would seem to be representations of choruses. The degree of theatrical realization for any concept of a chorus must remain uncertain; but it was clearly ambitious, and titles such as *Clouds, Transport Ships,* and *Islands* would seem to confirm a reliance on something more than costume (as clothing) for the effect.

In later comedy, beginning in a tendency noticeable by the end of the fifth century and confirmed in the fourth, the role given to the chorus diminished rapidly. In the comedies of Menander there is no written script for choral song, merely a notation that a chorus performed at four points in the play, dividing what would now be called five acts. In Aristophanes' early comedies the chorus helps to define the play, often as a visual joke and by close involvement in the action of the play; by the time of Menander the chorus provides only a subsidiary entertainment, totally disjoined from the actors.

There is some reason to believe that the satyr play was introduced to maintain a strong Dionysiac element in dramatic production. Satyrs were closely associated with Dionysus, and the development of tragedy toward a wide range of mythical subjects may have prompted the introduction of a form that by convention, in the unchanging nature of its chorus, ensured a tribute to the god in whose name the festival was undertaken. The one complete text of a satyr play that survives, Euripides' *Cyclops,* taken with the visual evidence of the vase painting of the cast for a satyric production (*DFA,* fig. 49; *HGRT,* fig. 20), provides a relatively firm picture of the entertainment involved. The satyric chorus would be expected to dance and sing (plate 3), and might well be active in the course of the play.

The choice of a chorus for dramatic performances is known to have been the responsibility of the *choregos,* but there is no firm evidence for the methods of selection used during the fifth century.

25

◙

ACTORS

THE ORIGINAL ACTOR in tragedy was the composer, and initially there was only one. The early plays of Aeschylus seem to require only two actors, and ancient sources state that Aeschylus was responsible for the introduction of the second performer. Aeschylus produced the *Oresteia* in 458 B.C., and for that trilogy three actors are required. Sources ascribe the introduction of the third actor either to Aeschylus or to Sophocles, who first won the tragic prize in 468 B.C.. The confusion is easy to explain if the innovation came at some time during that decade, when Aeschylus and Sophocles were active together. In 449 B.C. a competition was begun for the leading actors of each of the year's three tragic presentations at the City Dionysia. Probably before this time the practice of composers performing in their own works had ended: Sophocles was the first to make this decision, and it may well have come alongside the introduction of the third actor.

26

The Greek word for actor was *hypokrites,* which probably meant "answerer" originally: the composer, in taking a part in performance, is extremely likely to have "answered" the chorus. The evidence suggests that from the beginning, the actor predominantly spoke, although acted parts in the earlier plays of Aeschylus may have required singing. It seems extremely likely that he spoke verse, which initially must have been delivered either to the chorus or directly to the audience. One tradition ascribes the invention of the spoken parts of tragedy to the first named composer, Thespis, and this seems perfectly plausible.

One actor, with the aid of a selection of masks and costumes and the resource of a *skene,* might take several roles. The original advantages of a second performer are not so easy to determine: the obvious thought, for those influenced by later forms of drama, is the possibility of dialogue between actors as characters, known in later Greek terminology as *stichomuthia.* But, in fact, the earlier plays of Aeschylus show relatively little use of dialogue between actors. The principal reason for this is the direct relationship that most characters have to the chorus, or—to express this more precisely—the emphasis placed in these early plays on the reaction of the chorus to any communication made to it by a character. A growing complexity in the diversity of roles, and the advantages of a greater flexibility in the introduction or removal of characters, seem ultimately the most likely explanations for the innovation. Simple strain on the voice and physique of the composer-performer as roles increased may also have been a factor.

For two-actor tragedy, the division of roles would be a relatively simple problem, and it is not really possible to detect any striking imbalance in demands made on either performer. This is perhaps because there are only three plays of Aeschylus which appear to demonstrate this early two-actor form—*The Persians* (472 B.C.), *Seven against Thebes* (467 B.C.) and *The Suppliant Maidens* (463 B.C.)—and these all come from separate productions.

In Aeschylus' *Oresteia* trilogy of 458 B.C., a group of three surviving tragedies, three actors are required, with the possible momentary addition of a fourth in the second play, and the diversity of roles poses far greater problems for their attribution to individual actors. But the certain demands on all three performers are remarkably even, and the introduction and removal of characters throughout the trilogy could allow the same performer to play the same characters in successive plays, and the same actor to play both father and son, mother and daughter. The advantages of this system of association are obvious, in a form so heavily dependent on the voice, and it was perhaps employed.

In the other surviving tragedies, all of which may well belong to the period after the actors' competition was instituted in 449 B.C., it is important to notice the regular presence of a leading character, whose prominence in the action of a play would almost certainly have justified the attribution of that role to a leading actor, who was in competition with other leading actors. The need to gratify actors and audience with prominent roles may have dictated this emphasis. Otherwise, it would seem that the demands on tragic performers remained very much the same throughout the century, with the occasional requirement for extended singing, often in conjunction with the chorus.

The usual allocation of actors in tragedy was three, though *Alcestis* (438 B.C.) and *Medea* (431 B.C.) by Euripides might with some difficulty be acted by two, and there are some occasions when four seem to be needed (Aeschylus' *Libation Bearers* in his *Oresteia,* mentioned above, and Sophocles' *Oedipus at Colonus*). The limitation to three as a normal practice may be no more than pragmatic, and perhaps a result of the difficulties of identifying different speakers in a convention using full head masks. In addition, there may be nonspeaking masked characters, speaking or singing children, and almost any number of supernumeraries.

Conclusions about comic performance in the fifth century are largely limited to Aristophanes. Comedy seems able to use more than three masked actors, although an assumption of three would account for the substance of many of the surviving plays. The demands made on comic actors were inevitably very different from those made on tragic performers, and it is extremely unlikely that the same men would play in both forms. Aristophanic comedy is active, places a far more telling emphasis on dialogue and timing, and though it may throw one character into verbal prominence, many of its effects are achieved through physical routines, involving two or more characters, or character(s) and chorus. The capacity for acknowledged audience address, an abusive familiarity, mimicry, and the ludicrous qualities of many solo songs again distance the demands of the form from the relative consistency of tragedy. There was no prize for comic acting at the City Dionysia until late in the fourth century, though there was at the Lenaea from about 440 B.C., where there was also a prize for tragic acting.

The names of a few actors are preserved from the fifth century, along with the information that the playwrights made regular use of particular performers. Aeschylus is said to have had firstly Kleandros and then in addition Mynniskos as his performers. Whether Aeschylus acted all his life is not clear: the demands posed by any of the leading roles in the *Oresteia* would seem to be formidable to a man in his sixties, but this may be a false impression. So there is just a possibility that we

may know the names of the cast for the *Oresteia* in 458 B.C.
(Aeschylus, Kleandros, Mynniskos).

In the written tradition Sophocles is associated with an actor called Tlepolemos; but a series of pictures on vases suggested to the scholar T. B. L. Webster the association of another performer with productions by Sophocles. The name
Euaion, son of Aeschylus, is placed next to that of Perseus on
a vase illustrating Perseus arriving to rescue Andromeda (*IGD*
III.2.1), and recurs on a second vase that can be directly linked
to a tragedy (*Thamyras,* now lost) by Sophocles (*IGD* III.2.9).
The likelihood is that Euaion was an actor, and since Sophocles
wrote an *Andromeda,* as well as *Thamyras,* the association
seems certain. Written tradition records that Sophocles himself
acted the part of Thamyras, which required him to sing and
play the lyre; and on the painting Euaion's name is placed next
to that of an elderly woman, who is probably to be identified
with Argiope, the mother of Thamyras. The play will have
been relatively early, since later Sophocles stopped acting, because of weakness in his voice.

All the actors, as well as all the chorus members, for all three
forms of play, were men.

◼

THE PLAYING SPACE

THE PLAYING SPACE for early tragedy will have been the flat
ground of an *orchestra*. With the construction of a *skene* in the
theater of Dionysus, it is clear that some characters appear
from it, and that characters may enter it. Reappearance and
reentry are also common.

In principle, the chorus arrives in the playing space from
one or both of the two side paths (*parodoi* or *eisodoi* in Greek),
and only leaves the playing space at the end of the play. This

convention is on occasions broken, with the chorus temporarily leaving the *orchestra* by a side path in a few plays; and in two other striking examples the chorus first appears from the scene building (Aeschylus' *Eumenides,* the third play of the *Oresteia* trilogy), or enters into it to reappear during the course of the action (Euripides' *Helen*).

How far the action of the plays was confined to the *orchestra* is problematic. Before the construction of a *skene,* and with no reference to a door, there is little alternative. In Aeschylus' *Persians* (472 B.C.), the Queen of Persia arrives in a chariot, and in the early plays most characters arrive in the playing space from "elsewhere," apparently from side paths. In these plays the fixity of the chorus, especially when combined with a leading character bound to them by ties of respect or obligation, seems to act as strongly as any other explicit information in a definition of locale. Characters appear to them, or with them, and may leave them; but it is the intensity of their experience far more than any impression of a closely defined space which controls our understanding of the action.

With the construction of a *skene,* this perhaps longstanding convention is bound to be partly broken. From the earliest scenic tragedies in the *Oresteia* the presence of a building is clearly marked, and the implications of residence are from then rarely absent. Even in the case of a temple, which is a repeated setting for tragedies, the introduction of the priestess or the god, or, in the hands of Euripides, the temple attendant (in his *Ion*), ensures a firm acknowledgment of the material existence of the scene building. It may be temporarily ignored, or, as in the case of comedy, readily redefined; but its existence nonetheless becomes the principal means of determining locality.

By the time of Menander, the *skene* had three doors, and regularly realized its capacity as a facade to unify the action between two neighboring houses. The conception linking all the surviving plays of Menander is one of lateral connection:

the space outside the doors is public, and there is no communication with a chorus. Characters remove themselves before
the chorus arrives to sing, and only reappear afterward.

The problem in determining a standard practice for scenic
performance in the fifth century has largely rested in the degree
of attraction that the body of surviving work is understood to
have to either the lateral convention (as in the works of Menander) that comes after it, or to the orchestral convention that
clearly precedes it.

As late in the fifth century as the production of Sophocles'
Philoctetes in 409 B.C. two characters open the play with no
explicit reference to the scene building. They appear from a
side path together, and the opening lines, spoken by Odysseus,
identify "this" as the shore of the island of Lemnos. A short
time later, a search is started for the mouth of a cave that
catches the sun, and one of the two finds it.

The compelling interpretation of this opening unites the
play far more firmly with what I have termed the orchestral
convention than with the urbane, "street-side" convention of
Menander. There is really very little to suggest, in any one of
the surviving dramas of the fifth century, that the action of a
play was confined to the immediate physical background of the
facade presented by the scene building.

Tragedy repeatedly makes use of what are obviously the
main doors of a scene building. With the existence of an *ekkuklema,* certain actors who are prone (such as Heracles in Euripides' tragedy of that name) must lie on it. Those who appear
beside the corpses it regularly carries may stand on it, or on
the platform that probably supported it. Alternatively, they
may come forward, to argue to (or with) the chorus. Proximity
is not always to be assumed in the Greek theater, and if assumed it may still vary widely in what was a massive playing
space. Nor should appearance from the scene building presup-
pose a rooting to the spot. Clytaemestra appears to welcome

Agamemnon, in an address to the chorus, in *Agamemnon,* the first play of the *Oresteia.* But Agamemnon has arrived in a chariot, and has not set foot from it. We need not suppose that she shouted to them all from a distance.

32   Comedy regularly redefines its playing space in the course of a play. So in *Acharnians* by Aristophanes the setting is first of all on Pnyx hill in Athens, with doubtless the audience cast in their other capacity as political assembly. But the setting fluently shifts to the house and home of the leading character, understood to be in "the country," since he proceeds immediately to celebrate the rural festival of Dionysus. Our scripts as records of performance can be awkward to read, for as a rule there are no original stage directions in them. But properties, people, and even painted indications of setting may all be removed in the space that, for us, separates one line from another.

The details of the action of any play may need to be deduced, and the scripts provide a wealth of detail on occasions. But they were not composed for deduction, and deduction can encounter the most frustrating obstacles. In Aristophanes' *Wasps,* all seems well. The old man, who is trapped in the *skene,* with the doors barred and a net stretched over it, tries to escape from a window. He has previously appeared on the roof, attempting to escape through the chimney; and our sense of the deployment of the *skene,* if not of its exact shape and appearance, is very strong in this play. But once he starts to climb down from the window, the indications in the script of physical activity become obscure (lines 430–60). It is clear that he is finally caught and held; that someone is instructed to climb up another way and beat him back; but who is where when, whether there is another window, when he is caught, all of which must have been exact in performance and obvious in presentation, are questions that cannot be immediately answered with any great confidence.

Some action will always have occurred by the door. For

comedy, other problems remain. There is only one house and one pair of doors (a double door is almost certainly entailed by the existence of an *ekkuklema*) in Aristophanes' *Wasps,* performed in 422 B.C.. One year later, with the production of Aristophanes' *Peace* in 421 B.C., sees scholars suggesting a radically different picture of the *skene,* in anticipation of the form with three doors available to Menander a century later. Tragedy, without exception it seems, used only one (central) door. The use of two (on either side of a third) or three doors is a presupposition for comedy in the later period, and seems so firmly attached to the comic form that it is likely to be an invention of it. Aristophanes' *Women in Assembly* of the early fourth century dramatizes neighbors. With a wooden *skene,* even above stone foundations, adaptations are possible. The comedies of Aristophanes after *Peace* and before *Women in Assembly* (*Birds, Lysistrata, Women at the Thesmophoria,* and *Frogs*) show absolutely no dependence on three doors. Either construction preceded persistent realization, or what confronts us in these plays of Aristophanes is evidence of a tendency that only finally dictated to permanent construction. There is no easy answer; but it must remain indisputable that the conception of most plays in the fifth century required only one entrance, which could on occasions be redefined in the course of a play.

◻

THE AUDIENCE

THERE IS contradictory and confusing evidence on the composition of the audience for the dramatic festivals. The capacity of the *theatron* will have varied with its gradual extension, but a figure of between ten and fourteen thousand seems a reasonable generalization.

Athenian society in this period was conscious of quite firm

categories, and amongst these adult citizen males held a dominant place in political, legal, military, and domestic affairs. Women were excluded from most aspects of public life, and slaves were regarded as one category of "things owned" by those who were "free." A large class of residents was formed by the "metics" (*metoikoi*), those Greeks who were immigrants to Athens or who were not of Athenian descent, and who did not have the full rights of citizens. It is perfectly possible that there were no rules affecting or controlling attendance at the theater, but the likelihood must be that of all the categories Athenian women and slaves would be the least in evidence. Visiting non-Athenians, particularly those acting as representatives of allied states, would have been present at the City Dionysia.

Athenian democracy, which was established at the end of the sixth century, and fully confirmed by the time of the *Oresteia*, attributed power to the people (*demokratia* combines "people," *demos*, with the concept of "power," *kratos*, in one word) in two decisive ways. The *demos* was effectively understood to be the totality of adult citizen males, and this body met in the political assembly (*ekklesia*) on the hill called Pnyx in Athens, to decide what we should call matters of state (*ta politika* in Greek, matters affecting the *polis*, or city/state), often with a strong military bias. The democracy also provided law courts, *dikasteria*, at which a representative selection of citizens would be the final arbiters in a majority of legal decisions.

It is important to realize that both these vital sectors of the political form taken by Athenian democracy relied on public speaking to a large audience, with a view to persuading a majority. The courts were composed regularly of five hundred *dikastai*, or jurymen, and attendance at the political assembly was supposed to be an obligation for all adult citizens. "Hearing," with a view to final judgment, was of the essence of Athenian democracy, and urgent persuasion the objective of public speaking. In this respect the shape of the political assembly is of considerable relevance in any accurate assessment of the activity of theater, and I have included diagrams of it (figs. 4a and 4b). A gently sloping embankment of different orientations in different periods was created to facilitate the reception and identification of speakers, and the analogies with the theater are plain (figs. 3a, 3b with 4a, 4b). Conversely, theaters were on some occasions, particularly during times of political instability, used as political meeting places. The connection between the theater and political life was far closer in Athenian life than it has been in modern times.

The expectations, reactions, tastes, feelings, and judgment of a relatively well-known audience of predictable scope must have affected the composition of plays to a very high degree. The allocation of prizes in the dramatic competitions seems to have worked by immediate and probably vociferous public pressure on a panel of ten judges, only finally selected just before the contest. From the verdicts of these men a majority was apparently achieved by a random selection of five out of ten. The procedure was clearly designed to safeguard the decisions from dishonest external influence. Some of the results of this system are known, and provide part of a picture of the general critical reaction. Aristophanes was disappointed by the audience reaction and the decision of the judges in relation to *Clouds,* which he proceeded to revise, commenting in the revision that he had seen the first version as intellectually the most "sophisticated" of his comedies. The text that survives of *Clouds* is a revision which was never presented, and which itself makes reference to the first production. Sophocles is said always to have been placed first or second in the tragic competition, but never third; Euripides won very few victories; and the Athenians voted a decree after the death of Aeschylus permitting reproduction of his tragedies in the place of new work. These judgments are interesting; but they leave us with only

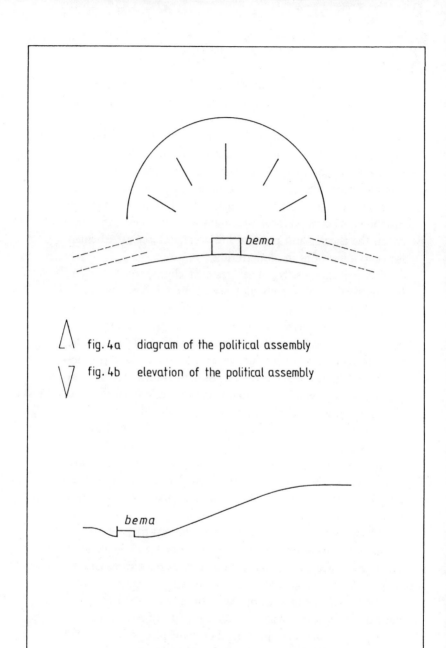

fig. 4a diagram of the political assembly

fig. 4b elevation of the political assembly

the barest indications of emotive response, or of the usual or varying criteria for critical appreciation or disapproval over the century. A comic distortion of critical judgment is presented by Aristophanes in his *Frogs* of 405 B.C., following the death of Euripides; but the contest in the underworld between Aeschylus and Euripides is simply and consistently irreverent, when it is not sentimental.

If it is impossible to determine with any accuracy what the Athenians thought or felt in detail about any play on any particular occasion, there are nonetheless some general controls on a modern assessment of what was presented to them. Two examples taken from the fabric of social life will illustrate this well. Athenian democracy gave a remarkable emphasis to the initiatives and obligations of the *kyrios* (literally "master"), the adult male who was legally responsible for all his dependants, and who was effectively the element of political and public life. A great deal of surviving Athenian drama reflects an interest in the *oikos* ("household"), seen as subject to the control of the *kyrios;* and a permeation of this concern into a world shaped by myth or fantasy provides much of the tension or humor apparent in many plays.

The second example is material, rather than thematic. The design of the larger Greek houses was traditionally based around an *aule,* or courtyard, from which entrances opened into the various parts of the house. The central doors of the *skene* are clearly taken to represent the main door to the courtyard in many plays where a "palace," or larger private house, is involved. Characters can often be assumed not to pass others— nor even, in some cases, to know what is happening in a different part of the house—when they go through them. A temple would also be understood to have sizable interior divisions of space, familiar in some form to most of the audience, and which could include some areas inaccessible to all but the cult priest/esses. This expands our conception of interior space in these plays, to an extent that would clearly not be so significant when the *skene* represented an inhabited cave, or a military tent.

Between the modern reader and the ancient script lies the audience for which it was composed. This is not an insuperable barrier, but as many adjustments as possible should be made before any "reading" is allowed to become completely convincing. Of all these, perhaps the most telling is that of repeated military activity as an inevitable definition of the adult male, and as a potential and catastrophic influence on the lives of others.

◧

DELIVERY

OF ALL THE ASPECTS of the actor's technique in the Athenian theater, that of delivery stands out as being thoroughly characteristic of a convention which relied heavily on the voice. The absence of facial expression made increased attention to voice and gesture inevitable, and confirmed a major distinction from standard forms of public address, in the political assembly or in the law courts. But despite this crucial difference, the analogies between the three forms were striking, and theoretical writers applied a term derived from the existence of acting to the projection that should be given to speeches, which they called *hypokrisis*.

There are no handbooks on the actor's technique, nor is anything known of rehearsals. But it is possible to mark out from the scripts certain fairly clear signs of the demands placed on a performer by the particular convention.

In Aeschylus' *Agamemnon* Clytaemestra eventually reappears from the *skene* to display the corpses of Agamemnon and Cassandra, whom she has murdered. At this point, she takes pride in announcing that the achievement of what she had intended may now be revealed in stark contrast to the manner of her previous statements (lines 1372–79). Earlier in the play, she has greeted Agamemnon with an effusive speech of welcome, assembled from exaggerated flattery and a pretense of extreme concern for his safety (lines 855–913). Its extent had drawn an ironic comment from her husband, who said that her speech had equaled his absence, because both were very long (lines 914–16).

The most likely conclusion to be drawn from this sequence would be that in the original performance the actor was expected, and the script of the earlier speech drafted, to convey exaggeration and insincerity. The bearings suggested by this example can be confirmed by another. In Euripides' *Medea*, a woman character is again faced by the need to convince, and eventually deceive, a leading male character. Medea actively pleads with Creon, who is the king of the city in which she is resident, for a temporary reprieve from exile for herself and her children (lines 271–356). After Creon has granted her wishes and left, she acknowledges to the chorus that her behavior toward him was a form of flattery, designed to gain her ends and with a firm intention in mind. This intention proves to be the triple murder of Creon, his daughter, and her husband Jason (lines 364–85).

The activity of significant and extended deception allows for some of the clearest effects in the construction of Athenian tragedy, and was presumably intended and scripted for execution. The absolute alternative to active and acknowledged deception might be best seen in the sincerity of feeling which can be occasioned by deception. In Sophocles' *Electra*, Electra is given every reason to believe in the death of her brother, whose "ashes" are conveyed to her in an urn. The demonstration of her grief, which is extended (lines 1126–70), must provide for the play an extreme of sincere emotion, which stands in marked opposition to the hypocrisies determined by Aeschylus for Clytaemestra.

Most speeches, if not all, invite discrimination from the audience. Many are concerned with self-justification, because the figures seen are largely responsible for their actions, or, at least, for their immediate decisions. The portrayal of extreme sincerity or its opposite may have been one objective of the actor's technique, but there will have been others. In Sophocles' *Antigone,* the new king Creon appears from the *skene* to address the chorus. Before confirming the rigor of his recent proclamation forbidding the burial of his nephew Polyneices, killed one day earlier when attacking his own city, Creon is at pains to emphasize the continuing loyalty to the ruling house of Thebes of this élite of older citizens. They represent a tradition of respect and support across three generations of rulers already, he claims; they will, he imagines, support and respect him too, even in his early judgments. The proclamation in itself has demonstrated Creon's desire not to be thought to favor those close to him on his accession to power; and the delivery of this opening speech confirms his insecurity. On first public appearance, he is demonstrably willing to flatter those on whom he may have to rely to sustain him against public pressure (lines 162–222).

Of all the forms of delivery which may seem most obvious to the modern reader that of the portrayal of anger might encourage the greatest certainty. Words for anger are pointed in the script, and an accumulation of insult can offer firm signs of its presence in delivery. So in the exchange between Creon and Teiresias, the blind prophet, which occurs later in the same tragedy by Sophocles, the insults of Creon leveled at Teiresias prompt a slow rise to a prophecy of destruction directed at the king—as Teiresias himself acknowledges—like an arrow from a bow. The growth in intensity in clearly marked stages, and under explicit provocation, is in this case almost decreed by the composition of the script (lines 1033–90).

But two further examples from the same play offer interesting insights into the control that composition seems to place on delivery. In the opening exchange between Antigone and Ismene, two sisters whose diverse reactions to Creon's proclamation form the introduction to the action of the play, the intensity of conflict only certainly includes the direct expression of anger at its climax, when Ismene refers to the "heated" resolution of her sister (line 89). And later, at the first suggestion of opposition to his authority, and of the possibility that contravention of his proclamation may have been the result of intervention by a god, Creon orders the chorus to be silent, before they fill him with anger by further developing that suggestion (line 280). These examples are a warning that conclusions about delivery should be monitored, as far as the script is informative, by an acceptance of dramatic construction. Production and direction, and the full implications of composition, will have been as significant as any striking possibilities for immediate expression on the part of the performer.

In comedy, certain conclusions present themselves as almost inevitable, though since they are dependent on comparison they remain poorly defined. Aristophanes' *Women at the Thesmophoria* makes particularly heavy use of the technique of parody, deployed by Aristophanes in a variety of forms, but rarely when a surviving song or tragedy permits us a direct comparison (see the section "Parody" below). In *Women at the Thesmophoria,* a relative of the tragedian Euripides has infiltrated the women's religious festival identified in the title in order to defend Euripides from attacks the women will make on the subject matter of his plays. The relative is discovered and caught, and he and Euripides act out "escape" motifs from some of the playwright's tragedies. By chance, one of these ridiculous adaptations, or parodies, is from Euripides' *Helen,* a surviving play. This permits a comparison with the original, but more usefully for any understanding of delivery it draws attention to what must have been a particular resource of comic technique: a manner of indicating a certain type of tragic delivery while unmistakably rendering its ridiculous opposite. It also provides some confirmation that the male tragic performer will have modified his voice in representing women. The relative of Euripides is a man who has disguised himself as a woman to gain access to the festival. In representing Helen he can accomplish a parody of the tragic actor's realization of a woman as well as of the tragedy. This kind of vocal control may have been familiar from tragedy: the most likely division of roles for Sophocles' *Women of Trachis,* for example, would attribute the parts of both Deianira and Heracles to the same performer, which suggests disciplined flexibility rather than specialization.

   A further point of comparison for the techniques of delivery in comic performance lies in its use of characters drawn from contemporary life. This not only provided some interesting activity for the mask maker, but posed problems for the playwright and the actor. Euripides was alive when Aristophanes represented him in his comedies *Acharnians* and *Women at the Thesmophoria,* and so was Socrates for the original production of *Clouds* in 423 B.C.. But in respect to portrayal, and particularly to delivery, a more significant example is provided by the active political speaker Cleon, who is represented as the Paphlagonian slave in Aristophanes' *Knights.* What is interesting for our understanding of delivery in this play is that Cleon is known from another, reliably descriptive source (the historian Thucydides) to have been the "most violent" of contemporary public figures, and the most persuasive speaker. It is not unlikely that this description will have referred as much to his manner, his delivery in the assembly and elsewhere, as it did to his policies; and Aristophanes certainly chooses to represent him in that way, as far as the comments and expectations of other characters in *Knights* permit us to judge. The details of performance remain obscure, but the intention will surely have

42

entailed some representation by the performer, as one of the varieties of comic distortion.

One final observation should concern the descriptive reports given to messengers in tragedy. These extended speeches are often climactic, by their position in the play and by construction. A spoken description of major events will have been important in antiquity, and a vivid evocation often admired, perhaps best by those not directly affected, or by those immensely relieved by the news conveyed. Speeches of this kind in tragedy suggest a capacity for recall which should not be doubted in a society of this kind; and their subjects—disastrous accidents, a scene of explosive individual violence, or some part of the scale of a military engagement, to take three examples—are not unlikely topics for detailed descriptions. The composition and delivery of them in tragedy are artifices, as is often their contrived effect on a character carefully placed by the playwright to absorb their impact. The artifice will have been recognized by the audience; but it should not be assumed, in a modern reading, to have diminished their original theatrical excitement.

43

�▢

DISTANCE AND PHYSICAL ACTION

DETAILED STAGE DIRECTIONS are substantially an invention of the nineteenth century, and the scripts of ancient drama are a record of the words. But taken by themselves, the scripts still give some quite precise indications of physical action and of the use of space.

Direct physical contact firmly placed in the playing space provides a starting point for analysis, in either an embrace or a blow. In Aristophanes' *Frogs,* Dionysus and a slave, Xanthias, visit the underworld, and are alternately beaten by the ghastly doorkeeper of the palace of Hades, who is accompanied by slaves. All three speaking actors finally enter the *skene* (lines 605–73). The likelihood is that they are never far from the doors. By contrast, in Euripides' *Hecuba* the queen appears first from the tent of Agamemnon, which is the *skene,* leaning on a stick and supported by younger women as she moves slowly forward. In Euripides' *Heracles,* the name character is prostrate on the *ekkuklema* late in the play, next to the corpses of his wife and children. He covers his head with his cloak in shame at the approach of Theseus, who first instructs the third actor, playing Amphitryon, to unveil him, and then does so himself. Finally, in Euripides' *Ion,* the chorus has gathered close to the steps of the temple of Apollo represented by the *skene,* close enough to hear the sound of the doors opening. Wherever Ion may be standing, his supposed father then bursts out of the temple and attempts to embrace him. Ion is disgusted, pushes his hands away, and eventually threatens him with an arrow from the bow he is carrying (lines 517–24).

Prominent among other kinds of physical contact in tragedy are those moments when one character begs for a favor from another. In the exchange between Medea and Creon in Euripides' *Medea* (431 B.C.), Medea finally secures the reprieve she is seeking by a direct physical appeal to the king of Corinth, grasping his knees and perhaps then his hand (lines 324–56). This form of appeal is repeated by Euripides three years later, when in *Hippolytus* the nurse and companion to Phaedra first grasps her hand, and then falls to hold her knees in a successful attempt to learn from her the cause of her sickness (lines 324–36). At moments of this kind the immediate space between the performers is clearly defined, but their position in the wider playing space is left open to question. The problem facing the visual reconstruction of tragedy is to reconcile these two different areas.

Two further examples may go some way toward doing this. At the opening of Sophocles' *Oedipus the King,* what seems to be a large group of suppliants, composed of young children, old people, priests, and young men, has gathered close to the altars outside the palace of Oedipus, to appeal for his help against the plague. Oedipus appears from the palace to speak to them, and the exchange between him and the Priest of Zeus is finally curtailed by a signal from others placed further away that the third performer, as Creon, is approaching along a side path. Creon is seen to have a garland on his head, and is then within hailing distance of the king.

A similar kind of approach by Polyneices in Sophocles' *Oedipus at Colonus* introduces a third component of physical setting, open to a less close definition than contact or extreme distance, but vital to the action of many plays. Oedipus, old, blind, and homeless, has been carefully placed by the chorus in the early part of the play on the edge of a wooded sanctuary dedicated to the Eumenides. He is finally left on a "platform" of rock, for which the word used is the same as that for the speaker's platform in the public assembly (*bema*), and which undoubtedly indicates his presence at the edge of the supporting structure for the *ekkuklema*. He finds himself physically incapable of unaided movement (lines 501–2) and exhausted, and cannot leave the security of sanctuary.

Oedipus' daughters are grouped with him in this position as Polyneices makes his approach from a side path. He is seen at a distance by Antigone, is identified, and finally stands close enough to the actor playing Oedipus to describe his clothing and the details of his mask. He hesitates to address Oedipus directly, and speaks to his sisters instead, attempting to use them as intermediaries. His father turns away: they eventually speak to each other, but there are no indications of direct physical contact. The appeal that passes, at this close distance, from Polyneices to Oedipus is vehemently rejected (lines 1249–1413).

This kind of controlled proximity provides some of the most elusive problems in visualizing the action of ancient tragedy. Polyneices is held at a close separation from Oedipus that corresponds to the conflict between his need to make the appeal and his hesitation—and perhaps his revulsion—before the disfigured and ghastly old man, who is his brother as well as his father. Revulsion may take a different form: in Sophocles' *Philoctetes,* Philoctetes' wound seeps and is obnoxious, and his original isolation on the island of Lemnos was caused, at least in part, by disgust from others at the smell of it. But the whole action of Sophocles' play, which sees Neoptolemus sent to stay by him in the hope of stealing his bow, or of removing the man himself, is presented as a set of variations on the conflict between the impulse of approach and a sense of revulsion, of hesitation, or of suspicion that repeatedly acts to hold both men back. Extreme distance and immediate contact are the simplest deductions for a modern reader: but the tension of tragedy will have been regularly expressed in the careful description of an area enclosing two (or three) performers.

For comedy, the problems are of a different kind. Comic action is just that—active humor—and much of it is located around the doors of the *skene,*, or in a close relationship to them. The wider playing space is represented by interaction of performers—often violent—with the chorus, or by an almost ritual expulsion of other performers/characters, who are often introduced in succession along the side paths. The relationship to the *skene* of a similar physical concept may vary within an apparently slight range. For the opening of both *Clouds* and *Wasps,* two figures are trying to sleep outside. The two slaves of *Wasps* are placed close to the door, because they are supposed to be guarding it and not falling asleep. The two prone figures in *Clouds* are Strepsiades and his son, who eventually discuss a door which is at some distance. The revised text of the play seems to conceive of them as being at first "inside," and then later at a distance practicable for an approach to the school of Socrates. The slaves in *Wasps*, if they are to avoid being caught out and seen dozing by their owner, must keep close to the doors, because their owner is placed on the roof.

Other kinds of distance determine themselves effectively without the need for exactitude. Comedies, and comic routines, often compose themselves around objects, and one favorite device consists of the repetition of fetching a succession of thematically related objects from inside the *skene* out through the doors to a performer or performers firmly located outside. In *Acharnians,* a contrast is achieved between the self-indulgence of Dikaiopolis and the hard military life of Lamachus by having brought to each on order the equipment and provisions for a meal and for a military campaign respectively (lines 1071–1149). The two performers finally leave down side paths, so they will have been at a distance from the doors and presumably separated. In *Lysistrata,* Kinesias is seen and then identified from the scene building, approaching along a side path. He appeals to his wife to come down to him from the *skene,* and invites her to make love with him on the ground. The rest of the scene sees her teasing his frustration by continually entering the *skene* to bring out further comforts or enticements, which he claims he does not need. The routine is again repetition, and the action will have taken place at a sufficient distance from the doors for the visual effect of interruption to be registered successfully (lines 829–979). Kinesias finally leaves along a side path.

A larger number of performers may gather around an object

in a grouping only loosely connected with any definition given by the scene building. In *Lysistrata* and *Women in Assembly,* Aristophanes repeats the idea of a conspiracy of women in a public space. In the first comedy unity is provided by the wine-pouring as a preliminary to taking an oath of sexual abstinence; and in the second individuals practice the speeches they will make in the assembly by passing the speaker's wreath from one to another. Both meetings are called at dawn, and in both plays the *skene* is almost immediately used to justify the appearance of one of the conspirators. But in *Lysistrata* it is finally defined as the gate to the *akropolis,* and then approached and entered by some of the performers; while in *Women in Assembly* it retains its definition as a house for the following scene, as the women leave to go to the assembly. A central position for both groups, which are formed with one exception by approaches from the side, seems most likely; and perhaps for this reason the *skene* itself is temporarily ignored until its chosen redeployment.

48

▣

CHORAL SONG AND CHORAL ACTION

SOME FORMS of comic and tragic action draw performers into close involvement with a chorus which is extremely active, and which may dominate the playing space. This is particularly true of early tragedy, and of comedy. The standard assumption about the chorus is that it sings and dances. This covers a wide range of theatrical possibilities.

Not enough is known about the choral music of Greek antiquity to make a reconstruction of its theatrical value possible. The same is unfortunately true of dance, for the occasional illustration of members of a dancing chorus (plate 1) is obviously inadequate to picture a sequence, though some vases clearly do attempt to give a picture of dance steps or movements (plates 2 and 3). But some observations can be made on the construction of the choral song, and its involvement in the action of a play may be explicit.

A typical tragic choral song might be composed in five parts, on the system a^1, a^2, b^1, b^2, c. These systems are detected in the existing scripts by the fact that the organization of the verse meter corresponds for two parts (a^1, a^2), and then changes for the next two. The system may extend, and the internal length of the parts of it may vary. It may or may not be concluded by a part standing in isolation (c). The corresponding parts of a song are conventionally known as *strophe* (literally "turning") and *antistrophe* ("turning back"); but the original significance of these terms may well be musical, rather than choreographic. This is certainly the implication of a passage mocking musical composition (for tragedy) in Aristophanes' *Women at the Thesmophoria* (lines 66–69).

A good example of this kind of tragic song is represented by an ode (the Greek word for "song") in Euripides' *Hippolytus* (lines 525–64). The action of the play has seen the revelation of Phaedra's passion for Hippolytus, her stepson, and the initial shock felt by the nurse giving way to a plan on her part to cure Phaedra of this sickness.

The song exists in four parts (a^1, a^2, b^1, b^2) without the conclusion (c), and opens with a prayer to Eros, the personification of the impetus of passion, which occupies the first two parts (a^1, a^2—lines 525–44). The second two parts (b^1, b^2—lines 545–64) consist of examples taken from mythology of the drastic power of Aphrodite, the goddess identified with sexuality, to strike the lives of women violently. The whole song concludes, in the final lines of its fourth part, with an

image, comparing the potent universality of Aphrodite to the
flight of a bee (lines 563–64).

strophe

Love distills desire upon the eyes,   525
love brings bewitching grace into the heart
of those he would destroy.
I pray that love may never come to me
with murderous intent,
in rhythms measureless and wild.
Nor fire nor stars have stronger bolts   530
than those of Aphrodite sent
by the hand of Eros, Zeus' child.

antistrophe

In vain by Alpheus' stream,   535
in vain in the halls of Phoebus' Pythian shrine
the land of Greece increases sacrifice.
But Love the King of Men they honor not,   540
although he keeps the keys
of the temple of desire,
although he goes destroying through the world,
author of dread calamities
and ruin when he enters human hearts.

strophe

The Oechalian maiden who had never known   545
the bed of love, known neither man nor marriage,
the Goddess Cypris gave to Heracles.
She took her from the home of Eurytus,
maiden unhappy in her marriage song,
wild as a Naiad or a Bacchanal,   550
with blood and fire, a murderous hymenaeal!

antistrophe

O holy walls of Thebes and Dirce's fountain   555
bear witness you, to Love's grim journeying:
once you saw Love bring Semele to bed,
lull her to sleep, clasped in the arms of Death,
pregnant with Dionysus by the thunder king.   560
Love is like a flitting bee in the world's garden
and for its flowers, destruction is in his breath.

(translation by David Grene, in
The Complete Greek Tragedies)

The opening prayer (a¹) is clearly motivated by the recent understanding of Phaedra's passion, and takes a common form of a negative wish, that Eros may not strike the chorus badly, or out of rhythm (lines 528–29), which serves as a religious acknowledgment of the divinity of the power of Eros, joined to that of Aphrodite. Continuity in the second part (a²) follows easily from the matching meter: Eros is a divinity of great destructive potency, and it is futile for organized religion not to institute his worship. The understanding here is that rites of worship, commonly expressed in the sacrifice which links human to divine, are an effective appeasement of an immortal power. The second two parts (b¹, b²), which share a metrical pattern which is distinct from that of the first pair, though closely related to it, provide two separate examples: the one of Deianira (the Oechalian maiden) in a sexual union born of violence (b¹), and the second of Semele, who was destroyed by a thunderbolt in childbirth (b²). The stories of both women formed part of the repertoire of tragic myth, from which other surviving plays were composed (Sophocles' *Women of Trachis*, and, less directly, Euripides' *Bacchae*).

The structure of this song, which works through development as well as balance, its subject matter, and the timing of its intervention in the action of the play are all accessible; and with considerable variation it provides a comprehensible pattern for an integration of choral lyric into a modern reading of the tragedies. But the diversity of lyric is immense; and apart from the knowledge that choral song was accompanied by a piper (*auletes*) playing double pipes, regularly pictured on vases (e.g., *DFA*, fig. 35), our ignorance of its music and dance is a definitive limitation. Musical mode and melody, physical expression by the use of hands and arms, and varieties of dance step or scheme are all attested; but what is known of them hardly permits even a reasonable generalization for the fifth century. Appropriate distinctions were almost certainly made for tragedy, comedy, and satyr play, and these were presumably familiar to the audience by convention.

52

The existence of meter, and its explicit organization into schemes in the scripts, can easily dominate a consideration of the chorus. But there is an abundance of evidence in the plays which points to a remarkable fluidity in the deployment of the chorus as a body, which for discussion is perhaps best separated from the internal design of a song. The plays of Aeschylus seem to provide evidence of an extremely active chorus, easily defined as apprehensive (*The Persians*), simply terrified (*Seven against Thebes* and *The Suppliant Maidens*), or combative and violent (*The Eumenides*, the third play of the *Oresteia*). The fluidity of movement in these plays can often only be guessed, partly because of the extent of the choral part(s) in them, which is noticeably greater than that standard for the later tragedies of Sophocles and Euripides. Combative violence is also a characteristic of comic choruses in Aristophanes, and it is tempting to see comedy as more traditional than tragedy in its preservation of dramatic agitation in the orchestral playing space to a far later date. In this respect, a general scheme of the broadest relevance can be provided by a contrast between the involvement of the chorus in the activity of the play in Euripides' *Bacchae* and in Aeschylus' *Eumenides*. Both plays dramatize a ritual hunt of a leading male character by a female group, inspired by a religious force and intending to kill. In *The Eumenides,* the hunt is performed by the chorus; in *The Bacchae,* the hunt takes place outside the playing space and is not performed by the chorus, although they are devotees of the god concerned, who is Dionysus. They remain in the playing space, and their songs express a combination of religious intensity and vicarious excitement, in the anticipation or reception of acts initiated by others.

The Eumenides provides a good example of choral action. The chorus first appears from the *skene* itself and apparently singly. The full group is composed still close to the *skene* when they are banished from the temple it represents by the god of the sanctuary, Apollo. They leave the *orchestra,* go down a side path, and arrive back again in the playing space, in an enactment of a successful search for the actor playing Orestes. This series of actions is expressed verbally, in both speech and song.

The exact location of the chorus in the playing space is nearly always hypothetical, and often dependent on the location of an actor or actors with whom the chorus is immediately involved. The search for Orestes in *The Eumenides,* for example, may range through the *orchestra* and culminate by the *skene,* where he is discovered. We deduce his presence there from the statue of the goddess Athene which he is clasping in the hope of asylum, since the statue may very well be located on the *ekkuklema* in front of the *skene* doors. The problem can be usefully seen in Euripides' *Suppliant Women.* At the opening of the play one actor is lying, collapsed, in what is later identified as the "porch" of the temple represented by the *skene,* and which will have been the platform in front of the doors. With him is a group of children. A second actor is apparently sitting by an altar, or altars, and surrounded, in what is explicitly stated to be a circle, by the chorus. The full theatrical complement is then completed by the arrival of the third actor, along a side path, who seems to see the choral group first and the actor and boys in the porch later, though this sequence may not be significant. The problem is complicated by the fact that there are two possible locations for an altar in the playing space: the first by the side of the *skene* doors, and the second in the center of the *orchestra,* where ancient sources place an altar to the god of the festival. In this particular case, the distinction in the script between the two separate groups suggests an orchestral location for the altar.

For comedy, a link to the tragic chorus is provided in the hunt or search, which also seems to have been a regular activity for the satyric chorus. In a large number of later plays, and in part in the tragedies of Aeschylus, the arrival of the chorus, with chant or song, is motivated by an attraction to the location as defined by the *skene,* or to a particular character either known or expected to be in the playing space. In Euripides' *Suppliant Women,* one extreme is represented because the script of the play opens as a description of the elaborate display in front of the audience. The most likely conclusion here must be that when the players enter the playing space before the beginning of the scripted action, they will have done so in silence. The alternative extreme can be illustrated, in comedy, by the chorus for Aristophanes' *Acharnians,* who arrive in detestation and violent pursuit of a character whom they regard as a traitor. He has, in fact, escaped into the *skene,* and their initial search must cover the *orchestra,* after their approach has been forcibly established in advance by a character arriving at a run from a side path. The attack on the "traitor" takes place when he has reappeared from the *skene* and enacted a procession with members of his family. From the moment of attack, the family finds no further mention in the script. The procession, the disappearance of the family group and most of the properties they are carrying, and the isolation of the one main character, apparently prevented from reentering the *skene* or escaping along a side path, place the attack firmly in the *orchestra,* where the full scope of twenty-four performers threatening just one would be seen to best advantage.

In general, a close association of the chorus with the *orchestra* seems inevitable apart from moments of explicit reference to the *skene*—such as, for example, the entry of the chorus into it in Euripides' *Helen.* There is no clear understanding of the playing space, in continuity of design or conception, that can consistently locate choral song and action anywhere else. If this is the case, then interaction between chorus and characters must be visualized as drawing actors into the *orchestra* as readily as it draws chorus to actors initially or apparently located by the *skene.* How the chorus may have been dispersed in the *orchestra* when addressed by characters or involved, at least partially, in exchanges with or between them is another problem, which does not seem to be susceptible to generalization. The complete perimeter, particular areas within it, and the possibility of marked divisions of a chorus in the playing space, sometimes apparent in characterization (Aristophanes' *Lysistrata* has a divided chorus of old women and old men), are as likely as components of the total convention as any major, single grouping close to the *skene.* A chorus positioned here rapidly becomes theatrically implausible: it will have to pull back to sing and dance in the *orchestra,* and will interrupt or visually inhibit the transit of actors from *skene* to side path or the reverse.

The tradition that the tragic chorus sang in three linear ranks of five, constructed in a block formation, comes from later antiquity, and would appear to be contradicted by explicit indications in at least some of the scripts. It cannot be true of the first appearance of the chorus in *The Eumenides* (458 B.C.), and seems totally irreconcilable with the description of the "circle" in Euripides' *Suppliant Women* (later 420s B.C.). A similar construction for comedy also seems highly implausible as a general rule, and is explicitly contradicted in Aristophanes' *Women at the Thesmophoria* (lines 953–68) of 411 B.C.. But there is no reason to suppose that the chorus for tragedy did not sing (and dance) in formation on appropriate occasions, perhaps even regularly so after its initial appearance (plate 1).

Certain sections of the script for the tragic chorus are differentiated metrically in a manner which does not indicate either song or the occasional involvement of chorus members in spoken exchanges between themselves or with actors. The usual assumption is that these passages were chanted, and there is at least a strong likelihood that they were accompanied by directional movement, rather than dance. Passages of this kind often introduce the chorus into the *orchestra,* and are then usually followed by the opening choral song. For comedy, a combination of short song with spoken or chanted harangue is repeated to form the *parabasis* of the chorus, which in its fullest form may have as a prelude a short call for attention, immediately followed by an extended (spoken or chanted) section which allows the poet to justify his work. Despite the strict formality of this sequence, and the certainty of accompaniment by the pipe player in some part (Aristophanes' *Birds* 676–800), the scripts generally reveal little of its presentation.

An actor or actors may also be involved in a system of song with the chorus, and this, for example, reaches degrees of considerable complexity in Aeschylus' *Libation Bearers* (lines 306–478). Varieties of this form might be a chant from an actor combined with song from the chorus, or with chant from the chorus. These distinctions are often hard to follow in translations, which are weak in their notation of theatrically quite distinct elements.

The separation of parts of a song by spoken sections is a relatively unusual feature of tragedy but a regular assumption for comedy, and tragedy may also, on occasions, make use of a repeated refrain.

◨

PARODY

THE RELATION of comedy to tragedy is an integral feature of theatrical activity in the fifth century, because throughout most of the century in performances at the City Dionysia, and from just before 430 B.C. at the Lenaea, Athenians were accustomed to a close association of the two forms (see above, "The Organization of the Festivals").

The degree of contrast between tragedy and comedy is explicit in the use made by Aristophanes of parodies of tragic language, mechanisms, and situations. Comedy is crude and colloquial, as part of its direct appeal to an audience; and mock solemnity achieved by the inclusion of lines from tragedies, or by the imitation of tragic language, is an immediate source of laughter. This recurrent technique can be extended to a parody of scenes, first mentioned above in connection with *Women at the Thesmophoria* (see "Delivery"). In that play, Aristophanes takes advantage of two tragedies presented by Euripides one year earlier, *Helen* and *Andromeda,* to burlesque the idea of escape. The recall of lines, part lines, or groups of lines from Euripides' *Helen* is clear to us because that tragedy (unlike *Andromeda*) survives; and Aristophanes places them in an inevitably free version of the reunion of Menelaus and Helen, which is interspersed with incredulous interjections from a third party and padded out with appropriate pseudo-tragic language and gross distortions of his own. Later in the same play he adds a further parody of *Andromeda,* which includes what must be a distorted version of a solo song by Andromeda and the arrival of the rescuing hero (Perseus), suspended, apparently, from the *mechane*. In both parodies, Aristophanes' comic caricature of Euripides plays the part of "his" male principals, and the captured relative lives up to the dramatic implications of

his impersonation of a woman at the women's festival of the
title.

Aristophanes' fascination with Euripides, which sees him
introducing the tragedian as a character in three of his surviving eleven plays (*Acharnians, Women at the Thesmophoria,
Frogs*), absorbs a great deal of his interest in the comic potential of tragedy. His attention is sophisticated: a ruthless parody
of Euripidean costume and properties in *Acharnians;* of the
"idle" use of the *ekkuklema* in the same play; of the *mechane* in
the opening of *Peace* and in the scene discussed above; and of
technical aspects of composition (introductions and solo
songs) in the contest between "Aeschylus" and "Euripides" in
Frogs. In both *Women at the Thesmophoria* and *Frogs* the parodies form the substance of the second half of the comedy; and
it is the theme of "Euripides" as tragic writer—deeply suspect
for his portrayals of female characters, or nostalgically recalled
after death—which forms the underlying conception of these
comedies. The same is also true, in part, of *Acharnians,* in
which Aristophanes seizes on certain striking characteristics of
Euripides' *Telephos,* a lost tragedy performed thirteen years before *Acharnians,* to lend shape to his comic action. Telephos
was the king of a region near Troy who was wounded in a
preliminary action against the Greeks, and he is compelled to
travel to Greece to get his wound healed. Although the substance of *Telephos* is lost, some fragments remain; and apart
from parodies of costume (a king in rags) and direct or reported action (the seizure of a child as a hostage, parodied
again in *Women at the Thesmophoria*), it is almost certain that
the comically provocative defense of Spartan conduct given to
Dikaiopolis in *Acharnians* reflects an attempt by Telephos to
justify the self-defense of "barbarians" against the Greeks. The
character of Lamachus, as the type of the general in *Acharnians*
and a foil for Dikaiopolis, is also likely to be a parody of the
type of the aggressive and single-minded Greek generals to
whom Telephos delivered his plea. Similar uncompromising

figures can be found by the modern reader in the characters of Agamemnon and Menelaus in Sophocles' *Ajax,* a tragedy which may have had an influence on Euripides' conception in *Telephos.*

It is, of course, true that parody in Aristophanes is not con-   59
fined to Euripides. "Aeschylus" is a leading character in *Frogs,* in which there are parodies of his introductions and his choral songs, alongside allusive mockery of his concept of tragedy and techniques of plot construction. In *Women at the Thesmophoria,* the recently successful young tragedian Agathon is introduced as a character not only to mock his personality—the *ekkuklema* is used again, as is costume—but to present a parody of the style of his songs (lines 101–29). *Wasps* concludes with the irrepressible juror ProCleon demonstrating his capacity to outshine some forms of tragic and possibly satyric dance, ascribed to named performers. *Lysistrata* concludes with what pretends to be a parody of Spartan forms of song and dance. In *Acharnians,* Dikaiopolis, in a comic account of the causes of the current war between Athens and Sparta, provides an unmistakable parody of the mythical causes of conflict between Greeks and Persians expressed in the introduction to the contemporary *Histories* of Herodotus, a prose work undoubtedly recited or read at Athens (lines 496–556). In *Birds,* the airy location of the newly founded city is seen to be a suitable venue for the vanities and conceits of the dithyrambic poet Kinesias (lines 1372–1409).

Much of Aristophanic comedy is concerned with what is topical, and this in part explains the presence of what we would call theatrical, musical, or literary parody in many of the plays; even in *Frogs,* which has a retrospective quality, Euripides is only recently dead. But the character of Dionysus in *Frogs* refers to his own reading of a tragedy by Euripides (the play is *Andromeda,* performed seven years earlier). It is clear from this as from other evidence that literary texts, including plays, were available for purchase in Athens from about that time; and there must always have been at least an official or inherited private copy for our scripts to have survived. There is an obvious irony in this passage from *Frogs,* since "Dionysus," of all the gods, might well be thought to take an interest in the past products of his own competitions—and as a god to have access to a script. But it does seem likely that Aristophanes would have had more than an acute theatrical memory—whether visual or verbal—to help him in recalling the texts of tragedies. *Acharnians* was produced thirteen years after *Telephos,* and allusions to that play suggest that Aristophanes might expect a significant proportion of his audience to be familiar with its action.

But apart from reading, or a reliance on sharp memory encouraged by humor, there is also the possibility of a repeat production of the original tragedy. This was permitted by public decree (after his death) for the plays of Aeschylus: a remarkable measure that was presumably necessary for a breach of precedent at a major festival like the City Dionysia, where work otherwise had to be original. But in the case of other writers any reproduction in the fifth century would have had to take place at the many lesser festivals of Dionysus in the townships or districts of Attica, or in a location such as Piraeus, the port of Athens. There was a theater in Piraeus by at least the end of the century, and certainly at Thorikos, in the southeast of Attica, from a much earlier date. Competitions for actors were established at the major festivals during the course of the century, and these may well have encouraged the spread of dramatic performances outside the city center, increasing familiarity with some popular plays. A growing professionalism among actors, with related developments, might readily provide a background for the later revivals of old plays at the City Dionysia itself in the fourth century. An increasing emphasis on the professionalism and consequently the mobility of the actor is also a likely reason for the decline of the chorus, which is a marked feature of comedy at least in the fourth century.

But as a comic technique parody is not confined to theatrical or literary sources. The great opportunity which tragedy provided for comedy was that it was a parallel performance, easily recalled, which might at times give substantial shape to the related resources of comic theater. This characteristic—of a public performance—was shared by many features of public life, which, because Athenian institutions were for most of the fifth century democratic, were perhaps almost tediously familiar to a majority of the audience. The mimicry and mockery that comedy displays draw our attention at times to this tedium, and offer a relief from it. There are parodies of the formulas of the political assembly (*ekklesia*) at the introduction of the chorus in *Women at the Thesmophoria,* and of speechmaking at the assembly in the introduction to *Women in Assembly.* Placed alongside the extensive mockery of the diplomatic agenda of the *ekklesia* at the opening of *Acharnians,* these add up to a sophisticated and varied exploitation of the same, totally familiar institution. The procedures and apparatus of democratic justice receive a similar treatment in the trial of the dog in the central part of *Wasps,* and the trite formulas of oracles, produced and used for political purposes, are parodied heavily in episodes from *Knights, Peace,* and *Birds.* Ritual, in the form of oath swearing (as in the introduction to *Lysistrata*) or even rural celebration (the rural procession in honor of Dionysus in *Acharnians*), offers possibilities for distortion or exaggeration; and individual characters may themselves contain the seeds of formulas of behavior or verbal expression.

This is true of Lamachus, who is the type of the soldier-general in *Acharnians,* with his jargon and equipment, and perhaps equally true of "Socrates," presented in a comic distortion of the intellectual teacher (sophist), with his terminology and instruments, in *Clouds.* But it may also extend to a collection of types, gathered around a recognizable occasion. In *Birds,* the newly founded city in the air is disturbed by the arrival of intruders. They number a priest, a poet, an oracle-monger, a surveyor, an *episkopos* (an Athenian imperial officer), a man who sells copies of laws and decrees, a choral composer, and an informer. All might readily be associated with the foundation of the new settlement, established as it is by renegade Athenians; and the sight and sound of them, and an absolute rejection of them as intruders, constitute a large part of the second half of the play.

Parody is not a concept that applies as readily to tragedy. But not all tragedy is absolutely serious, and critics have rightly drawn attention to elements of comedy in all three surviving tragedians. Perhaps the most accessible of these scenes is that between the shipwrecked hero Menelaus and a hostile doorkeeper in Euripides' *Helen:* itself, ironically, parodied by Aristophanes in *Women at the Thesmophoria.* But we should also add the ridiculous and pathetic appearance of the Phrygian slave from the roof of the *skene* toward the end of Euripides' *Orestes,* and the dressing of Pentheus in women's clothing in *The Bacchae.* There are comic precedents for both these scenes. In *Wasps* there is an attempted escape from the *skene* by Pro-Cleon, which occupies the introduction, and the "barbaric" language of the Scythian guard in *Women at the Thesmophoria* is to some degree echoed by the Phrygian slave. In both *The Bacchae* and *Women at the Thesmophoria* the careful clothing of a man is the preliminary to spying on women gathered in seclusion at a women's religious celebration. What evidence there is would seem to suggest that Euripides was as willing to create his own equivalent of parody in brilliant innovation for tragedy as was Aristophanes to mock him as innovator.

What the concept of parody when applied to tragedy may also allow us to do is to recognize conscious attempts at recall. The most famous of these lies in Euripides' radical transfor-

mation of the story of Electra in his tragedy of that name. Electra herself, in this play, refers directly and dismissively to techniques of recognition (of Orestes, her brother, by Electra) used
by Aeschylus in *Libation Bearers;* and this has suggested to
many the possibility of a reproduction of Aeschylus' trilogy,   63
the *Oresteia,* shortly before the presentation of Euripides' play
(about 420 B.C.). Euripides seems noticeably interested in the
work of others: *The Bacchae* is, apparently, a reworking of a
theme by Aeschylus, as is his *Suppliant Women* (of a lost trilogy
by Aeschylus), as perhaps is his *Iphigenia at Aulis.* In *The
Phoenician Women* the king Eteocles, in the climax to a review
of strategic options with Creon, dismisses abruptly the idea of
detailing the names of the captains who are to defend the seven
gates of Thebes against impending attack (lines 751–52). In
so doing, he removes from the audience the possibility of a
repeat of virtually the whole dramatic substance of Aeschylus'
surviving *Seven against Thebes.* In the same tragedy by Euripides, the introduction of the blind Teiresias to Creon and the
subsequent scene recall strongly to us, and perhaps did to some
of the Athenian audience, similar scenes between prophet and
ruler in Sophocles' far earlier *Antigone* and *Oedipus the King*
(*Phoenician Women,* lines 834–959). There is no explicit parody: but the familiarity that lies behind parody and the principle of reshaping for a sophisticated original purpose seem
closely related. The connection goes further: the dismissive references that we hear from Euripides' Electra and Eteocles may
confirm that Aristophanes was aware of "modernist" opinions
on dramaturgy (held against Aeschylus) actually expressed by
Euripides, which would account more than a little for the
theme of *Frogs.*

But the key to parody must be found in the audience, and
not in the playwright/composer alone. Familiarity with certain
forms, either theatrical or institutional, with their presentation
and the language appropriate to them, is clearly vital in sus-

taining and shaping both tragedy and comedy in the last quarter of the fifth century. The role of satyric drama in these relations is extremely hard to determine, except that the one complete surviving satyric play, Euripides' *Cyclops,* is obviously an adaptation of an episode narrated in detail in Book Nine of the epic poem the *Odyssey,* ascribed to Homer.

64

🔲

TRANSLATION AND ADAPTATION

TRANSLATION is, like theater itself, an art of presentation, and all translations bear the mark of their originators. Below are listed, as examples, some versions of the opening lines of Aeschylus' *Agamemnon;* they are spoken by the watchman.

Ye fav'ring gods, relieve me from this toil:
Fixed, as a dog, on Agamemnon's roof
I watch the live-long year, observing hence
The host of stars, that in the spangled skies
Take their bright stations, and to mortals bring
Winter and summer; radiant rulers, when
They set, or rising, glitter through the night.

(Robert Potter)

This waste of year-long vigil I have prayed
God for some respite, watching elbow-stayed,
As sleuthhounds watch, above the Atreidae's hall,
Till well I know yon midnight festival
Of swarming stars, and them that lonely go,
Bearers to man of summer and of snow,
Great lords and shining, throned in heavenly fire.

(Gilbert Murray)

The gods it is I ask to release me from this watch
A year's length now, spending my nights like a dog,
Watching on my elbow on the roof of the sons of Atreus
So that I have come to know the assembly of the nightly stars
Those which bring storm and those which bring summer to   65
men,
The shining Masters riveted in the sky—
I know the decline and rising of those stars.

(Louis MacNeice)

I ask the gods some respite from the weariness
of this watchtime measured by years I lie awake
elbowed on the Atreidae's roof dogwise to mark
the grand processionals of all the stars of night
burdened with winter and again with heat for men,
dynasties in their shining blazoned on the air,
these stars, upon their wane and when the rest arise.

(Richmond Lattimore)

Of the gods I ask deliverance from this toil, from my
year-long watch, in which, lying at the house of the Atridae
on my arms, dog-fashion, I have become familiar with the
assembly of the stars of night, and those bright potentates
conspicuous in the sky who bring winter and summer to
man.

(Eduard Fraenkel)

I've lain here a year,
crouching like a dog on one elbow,
and begged the gods to end my watch.
I've watched the stars. I know their comings
and goings, the bringers of winter and the bringers
of summer. The stars burn with power,
and rule their empty spaces like kings.

(Robert Lowell)

Dear gods, set me free from all the pain,
from the watch I keep, one whole year awake . . .
propped on my arms, crouched on the roofs of Atreus
like a god.

66

        I know the stars by heart,
the armies of the night, and there in the lead
the ones that bring us snow or the crops of summer,
bring us all we have—
our great blazing kings of the sky,
I know them, when they rise and when they fall . . .

                                     (Robert Fagles)

No end to it all, though all year I've muttered
my pleas to the gods for a long groped for end.
Wish it were over, this waiting, this watching,
twelve weary months, night in and night out,
crouching and peering, head down like a bloodhound,
paws propping muzzle, up here on the palace,
the palace belonging the bloodclan of Atreus —-
Agamemnon, Menelaus, bloodkin, our clanchiefs.

I've been so long staring I know the stars backwards, the
chiefs of the star-clans, king-stars, controllers,
those that dispense us the coldsnaps and dogdays.
I've had a whole year's worth so I ought to know.

                                     (Tony Harrison)

    Of these versions, that by Robert Potter is from the earliest English translation of the plays of Aeschylus, first published in 1777. Gilbert Murray was a scholar, whose versions of a number of Euripides' tragedies helped to bring Greek tragedy to the attention of London theater audiences at the beginning of this century. Louis MacNeice is the Irish poet, associated closely with W. H. Auden, and his translation was published in the thirties. Richmond Lattimore was a poet, and coeditor of one of the major postwar series of translations of Greek tragedy, published by the University of Chicago Press. Eduard Fraenkel was a scholar, who published (in 1950) an extensive edition of *Agamemnon,* which included a prose translation alongside the Greek text. Robert Lowell is the American poet, who wrote his version of this play in the early sixties. Robert Fagles' translation is published in Penguin Classics, the second of the major postwar series of translations of Greek plays; in the later seventies it replaced an earlier version by Philip Vellacott. Tony Harrison is an English poet, who wrote this version of Aeschylus' *Oresteia* for a production (in masks) by the National Theatre which opened in London in late 1981, and transferred to the Greek theater at Epidaurus in the following year.

The extracts given here are clearly too short for significant critical analysis, and represent only a selection, with a bias toward the later twentieth century; but they do provide an indication of variety, and of the problems facing translators. These will often vary according to whether the author is directing attention predominantly to a readership or to a live audience. At one end of the spectrum, a translation may be produced as an aid to close study of the original text, as was the case with Fraenkel. In versions of this kind the receiving language may risk some distortion in providing an equivalent of the patterns and distinctions of the original. On the other hand, as is the case with Harrison, a contemporary mode may be demanded for modern theatrical resources and conditions which will result in a relatively free version, or perhaps an adaptation.

The history of adaptation is of considerable importance in relation to some theatrical cultures. In France, Jean Racine adapted tragedies by Euripides for his *Iphigénie* and *Phèdre* in the seventeenth century; and in Germany Goethe, toward the end of the eighteenth century, turned to another play by Euripides for his *Iphigenie auf Tauris*. In the twentieth century both cultures have again shown a strong interest in Greek tragedy, with the plays of Cocteau (*La Machine Infernale*, drawing on the Oedipus legend), Giraudoux (*Electre*), Anouilh (*Antigone*), and Sartre (*Les Mouches, Les Troyennes*) in French; and those of Hofmannsthal (notably *Electra*) and the tetralogy on the house of Atreus by Hauptmann in German. In the United States a major impact was achieved by Eugene O'Neill with *Mourning Becomes Electra,* his adaptation of Aeschylus' *Oresteia*. In the British theater, the influence firstly of the Roman tragedian Seneca on Elizabethan tragedy and then that of Molière on the later restoration comedy have tended to stifle direct interest in Greek models, until the strong contemporary revival of Greek tragedies on radio and television, as well as on the stage.

The comments of those who adapt offer an interesting insight into the problems of translation. Looking back to the seventeenth century, for Racine Euripides was the most dominant of a number of sources, which he is at pains to acknowledge in his prefaces. In the preface he published to *Iphigénie,* he was conscious that he had distanced himself a little from "the economy and the plot of Euripides. But in so far as the passions are concerned, I have made every effort to follow him exactly." For *Phèdre*, his acknowledgment was couched in similar terms:

> Here once again is a tragedy whose subject has been taken from Euripides. Although I have followed a different path from that author in the conduct of the action, I have not failed to enrich my play with everything that struck me as most brilliant in his.

The emphasis here on the passions, and on what is "brilliant" or "striking" (*éclatant*) suggests a consistent concern for certain qualities of the original which may be distinguished from the actual language and construction of the play. This attitude is reflected in the modern period by comments from two further adapters, who develop their ideas in terms that are bound to be more familiar. The first passage is taken from observations made by Jean-Paul Sartre on his adaptation of Euripides' *Trojan Women,* performed and published in the mid-sixties; the second is by David Rudkin, in the foreword to his version of Euripides' *Hippolytus,* first performed by the Royal Shakespeare Company in Britain in 1978.

> There was an implicit rapport between Euripides and the audience for which he was writing. It is something which we can see but not share. Since this relationship was implicit, a translation cannot reproduce it. It was therefore necessary to adapt the play.
>
> (Jean-Paul Sartre)

> The reader—and spectator—may wish to know the relationship between this text and the original. I have rendered, line by line, not an abstract linguistic equivalent of the Greek, but what I understand its living significances to be. In matters of theology and myth (geography too), to us Greek references are practically meaningless. On the page, explanatory foot-notes can be provided. In the theater, we must know, in the drama's vital presence, what is actually being said. So must the actor. To achieve this, an interpretative commitment must be risked; an interpretation, though defined and governed by the letter of the text. A translation of a play is like a production of that play: it represents a moral response to it.

> The Greek dramatists are important. In the theater, I want to encounter what they are saying to me, not what they once said to someone else. Paradoxically, we might only ever approach the "original experience" of Athenian tragedy by first expunging from it every element we think of as

"Greek". Euripides' audience weren't watching a "Greek" play. They were watching a play of their own. So must we be.

(David Rudkin)

70   The promise of adapters is that the demands posed by theatrical performance will inevitably create a new, living theatrical work; but it may be equally possible that this script itself, once published, will be deprived of some of the vitality that performance brought to it. So we find that translations which are principally intended for a reading public will often record the particular details of the original without any marked attempt to adapt them. This is presumably because the distance of a translated work, in both time and language in the case of Greek drama, can be as important to some readers as its vitality across two cultures. Put simply, people may want to know "what was there" as much as they would like to experience "how it felt." And in some cases the adapters themselves, unless they know the original language, will have had to rely on translations. Seen from this perspective, there is no real contradiction between adaptation and translation: they simply serve different purposes.

The specific problems faced by translators of Greek tragedy occur largely in two areas, those of language and meter. Greek drama is composed, as was mentioned above ("The Writer" and "Choral Song and Choral Action") of spoken or chanted delivery and song, but the music and dance steps are missing. The problem is complicated by the fact that ancient Greek was an inflected language (spoken by pitch rather than stress), and so the metrical rhythm that can be seen in the text was only one of several influences affecting sound. But translators of tragedy invariably work by finding some equivalent rather than by discarding verse altogether; and a traditional solution has been to equate the spoken parts of the plays with the five-stress rhythm of English blank verse, since this is familiar to the ear from Elizabethan drama. Rhyme is not a feature of Greek drama, although it has appeared in some translations and adaptations (e.g., Murray, above). The complexity of rhythm in song has generally defeated the search for equivalents, and translators usually concentrate on language and clarity, since choral song is notoriously difficult to understand. But any rhythm translators into English do adopt will be based, however variably, on stress; and choral passages are usually marked out in translation by the simple expedient of shorter lines, largely a reflection of the way they are presented in editions of the original text.

The problems of language are immensely complex, and are resolved individually, as can be seen in the variety of even the small number of selections I have given from translations of *Agamemnon*. Typical obstacles for the close translator are limitations in the choice of verbal equivalents, lack of correspondence in expression between ancient Greek and English, and a discrepancy in the order of emphasis or construction in both languages. The original script obviously represents decisions by the particular author, and the pattern of these decisions may also vary over his lifetime, and from play to play. So there can never be "a model" for translating one of the dramatists, though there are separate arguments in favor of a diversity of translators (as in the Chicago series) or for one translator covering a body of work by one or more authors (as has regularly been the case in Penguin Classics).

Criticisms of translations will generally refer to "style," or, on occasion, to points of accuracy. Despite the apparently fault-finding quality of the second count, it is probably more valuable, since "style" is clearly close to taste and is a subject on which it is notably difficult to come to any firm agreement. In reviewing critical reactions to translations, it is probably fair to say that translators have generally succeeded less, and their translations been less long-lived or popular, when they have approached their work with a fixed sense of an established convention in poetry (or, perhaps worse, of an established convention in translation). The simple reason for this is that Greek drama obviously reaches behind any existing conventions in the reader's understanding to a historically remote period that a direct association with any period in the recent past is almost bound to disrupt. Those who write adaptations are perhaps particularly conscious of this (e.g., Rudkin), and Harrison came up with an interesting solution by pitching his version behind the main body of English literature into what he described as "ghostly Anglo-Saxon rhythms." The choices of an adapter will be open to critical reaction; but the moral they pose for translators is reasonably clear.

The comedies of Aristophanes have been far less widely adopted into modern languages and cultures than Greek tragedy, and the difficulties they offer for translators are complicated in particular by their insistent topicality, in jokes, subject matter, and allusions to contemporary figures. The sexual and excremental humor of Aristophanes did not encourage modern European versions, and where they existed they tended to be "bowdlerized" or censored. The sixties in the United States proved free from this inhibition, and the most vigorous translations probably date from that time. Translators generally discard verse forms for comedy, though British translators have a tendency to suggest Victorian or older "tunes" as a background accompaniment to some of Aristophanes' songs, which seems a strange association, and one which is rapidly losing whatever point it had. The range of existing translations is far less wide than that for many tragedies, but their diversity seems at least as great. Topical references (to personalities, events) and puns are two obvious problems in connection with laughter; and both are involved in the comprehensive difficulty of translating an intricate cultural context for the plays—involving political, artistic, legal, social, and religious institutions and assumptions—into a form which will carry both humor and conviction across to a modern audience.

The scale of some of these problems has seen criticism generally draw back from translations of Aristophanes, probably because it is felt that neither accuracy nor consistency of "style" are likely to be as significant as adroitness (or the lack of it) in re-creating humor. In other words, a translation is either "funny" or not. But this reaction may not be enough: Aristophanic comedy was certainly meant to make people laugh, but there is more to it than being simply funny. There would seem to be quite a strong case now for a distinction between free-handed versions and translations which permit close access without adaptation. One approach to the problem, adopted in the Penguin Classics series, is to append historical notes to a relatively close translation, and for certain purposes this is helpful. Probably the main obstacle to the successful translation of Aristophanes is, in fact, the lack of stimulating demand from the theater or other media. With the exception of *Lysistrata,* and on occasions *Frogs,* and apart from regular productions by the Greek National Theatre, there have been relatively few performances of Aristophanes' comedies, and few directly commissioned scripts. This has almost certainly dictated a lack of initiative.

Versions of some of the Greek plays exist on film, and the themes of the plays have had a far wider impact than their relatively direct reproductions in any one of the available contemporary media. This cultural vitality can only be assured by some continuing provision for study of the original language, which is most effective when it is linked to close attention to the originals as theatrical scripts. For readers or for audiences, renewed translation or adaptation will secure access to a body of work that has repeatedly demonstrated its appeal, most notably and widely in the twentieth century, and particularly in the period since 1945.

APPENDIX

Chronology of the Surviving Plays

The known dates are those of production. The positioning of other plays remains uncertain. (Ae.) = Aeschylus; (S.) = Sophocles; (E.) = Euripides; (Ar.) = Aristophanes.

472 B.C.	*The Persians* (Ae.)
467 B.C.	*Seven against Thebes* (Ae.)
463 B.C.	*The Suppliant Maidens* (Ae.)
458 B.C.	*Agamemnon, The Libation Bearers, The Eumenides* (the *Oresteia* trilogy) (Ae.)
?	*Ajax* (S.)
?	*Antigone* (S.)
438 B.C.	*Alcestis* (E.)
?	*The Women of Trachis* (S.)
431 B.C.	*The Medea* (E.)
?	*Oedipus the King* (S.)
?	*The Heracleidae* (E.)
428 B.C.	*Hippolytus* (E.)
?	*Andromache* (E.)
425 B.C.	*Acharnians* (Ar.)
424 B.C.	*Knights* (Ar.)
423 B.C.	*Clouds* (Ar.)
?	*The Suppliant Women* (E.)
?	*Hecuba* (E.)
422 B.C.	*Wasps* (Ar.)
421 B.C.	*Peace* (Ar.)
?	*Electra* (E.)
?	*Heracles* (E.)
415 B.C.	*The Trojan Women* (E.)
414 B.C.	*Birds* (Ar.)
?	*Iphigenia in Tauris* (E.)

?	*Ion* (E.)
412 B.C.	*Helen* (E.)
411 B.C.	*Lysistrata* (Ar.); *Women at the Thesmophoria* (Ar.)
?	*Electra* (S.)
?	*The Phoenician Women* (E.)
?	*The Cyclops* (E.)
409 B.C.	*Philoctetes* (S.)
408 B.C.	*Orestes* (E.)
405 B.C.	*Frogs* (Ar.)
?	*The Bacchae* (E.); *Iphigenia in Aulis* (E.)
401 B.C.	*Oedipus at Colonus* (S.)
391 B.C.	*Women in Assembly* (Ar.)
388 B.C.	*Wealth* (Ar.)

> *Prometheus Bound,* formerly attributed to
> Aeschylus, is of unknown authorship and date, as
> is *Rhesus,* attributed to Euripides.

The productions of *Lysistrata* and *Women at the Thesmophoria* in 411 B.C. will presumably have been at different festivals (Lenaea and City Dionysia).

All the plays of Aristophanes are comedies. *Cyclops* by Euripides is a satyr play, and his *Alcestis* is a play composed to take the place of a satyr play. The rest are tragedies.

GLOSSARY

agora	public meeting place, market, and sanctuary
akropolis	citadel
archon	magistrate
auletes	pipe player
bema	speaking platform
choregos/-oi	citizen(s) appointed to pay for the presentation of a *choros*
choros/-oi	singing and dancing group(s) of performers
didaskalos	(teacher), trainer, playwright/composer
drama	(action), a play
ekklesia	political assembly of citizens
ekkuklema	rolling platform
hypokrites	actor
kothornos/-oi	soft boot(s)
mechane	(machine), crane
orchestra	dancing floor
poietes	(maker), poet, playwright
prosopon/-a	mask(s)
prosopopoios/-oi	mask maker(s)
skene	(tent), scene building
theatron	theater, auditorium

BIBLIOGRAPHY

The bibliography is of works in English, although one or two of the books quote in Greek, without translation. The list is extremely selective, and is intended simply as a guide to some further reading.

SOURCE MATERIALS AND PHOTOGRAPHS

The abbreviations are those given in the text to identify illustrations.

HGRT = Bieber, M. *The History of the Greek and Roman Theater,* 2d ed. Princeton, 1961.

DTC = Pickard-Cambridge, A. W. *Dithyramb, Tragedy, and Comedy,* 2d ed. (revised by T. B. L. Webster). Oxford, 1962.

DFA = Pickard-Cambridge, A. W. *The Dramatic Festivals of Athens,* 2d ed. (revised by J. Gould and D. M. Lewis), reissued with a supplement. Oxford, 1988. Pickard-Cambridge, A. W. *The Theatre of Dionysus at Athens.* Oxford, 1946.

IGD = Trendall, A. D., and T. B. L. Webster. *Illustrations of Greek Drama.* London, 1971. Webster, T. B. L. *Greek Theatre Production,* 2d ed. London, 1970.

This introduction to the Greek theater, like most modern surveys, is indebted to the collection and evaluation of material by these and other scholars, though views on the interpretation of the evidence vary, and change over time. Two distinct, modern assessments of the problems surrounding presentation are those by J. M. Walton, *Living Greek Theatre: A Handbook of Classical Performance and Modern Production,* London, 1988; and P. D. Arnott, *Public and Performance in the Greek Theatre,* London, 1989.

80

GENERAL SURVEYS

Dover, K. J. *Aristophanic Comedy.* Berkeley and L. A., 1972.
Flickinger, R. C. *The Greek Theater and Its Drama,* 4th ed. Chicago, 1936.
Lesky, A. *Greek Tragedy,* 3d ed. London, 1978.
Norwood, G. *Greek Comedy.* London, 1931.
Reckford, K. J. *Aristophanes' Old and New Comedy,* vol. 1. Chapel Hill, 1987.
Vickers, B. *Towards Greek Tragedy.* London, 1973.

Comments on the usefulness of Dover and Lesky are given below ("Greek Drama"). Flickinger's is a thoughtful study, and Norwood is valuable for his comments on the older comic writers apart from Aristophanes. Reckford and Vickers both present stimulating and wide-ranging approaches to their subjects.

N.B. For the later comic writer Menander, the translation of plays and fragments in the Penguin Classics series is up-to-date, and includes a short bibliography.

GREEK DRAMA

Useful, short general surveys of Greek drama in the wider context of the surviving literature: K. J. Dover (ed.), *Ancient Greek Literature,* Oxford, 1981; and J. de Romilly, *A Short His-*

tory of Greek Literature, Chicago, 1985. Concise surveys of tragedy and comedy, including a catalogue-type discussion of the surviving plays: the books by Lesky and Dover (listed above, under "General Surveys"). For satyric drama: D. F. Sutton, *The Greek Satyr-Play,* Meisenheim, 1980; and the introduction by R. Seaford to his edition of Euripides' *Cyclops,* Oxford, 1984.

THE ORGANIZATION OF THE FESTIVALS

The standard work in English is the second edition of Pickard-Cambridge, *The Dramatic Festivals of Athens* (listed above, under "Sources"), reissued with a supplement in 1988. A more concise summary of the country and city festivals of Dionysus is given by H. W. Parke, *Festivals of the Athenians,* London, 1977 (country, 100–103; Lenaea, 104–6; City Dionysia, 125–36). K. McLeish, *The Theatre of Aristophanes,* London, 1980, has some helpful comments on preparations in his second chapter, "The Practical Playwright."

THE WRITER

The historical background to the skills required of the Athenian tragedians is the subject of the Sather Lectures by J. Herington, *Poetry into Drama: Early Tragedy and the Greek Poetic Tradition,* Berkeley and L.A., 1985.

THE THEATER

The standard work in English on the archaeological remains of the principal festival site is still Pickard-Cambridge, *The Theatre of Dionysus at Athens* (above, "Sources"). A more recent interpretation of the ruins can be found in J. Travlos, *A Picto-*

rial Dictionary of Athens, London, 1971. C. W. Dearden, *The Stage of Aristophanes,* London, 1976, is a specialized study of the problems relating to comedy.

82

SCENOGRAPHY

The best treatments of the circumstances surrounding the invention of scenography are to be found in surveys of Greek art: for example, M. Robertson, *A History of Greek Art,* Cambridge, 1981 (see index under Agatharchos, reputedly the originator of the art). Though written some four centuries after the plays, *On Architecture* by Vitruvius is the earliest surviving treatise of its kind. There is a parallel Latin/English text in the Loeb Classical Library: the observations on Agatharchos come at the beginning of book 7. A conclusion in favor of a limited number of standard sets is offered by N. C. Hourmouziades, *Production and Imagination in Euripides,* Athens, 1965.

MASKS, COSTUME, AND PROPS

A good range of pictures for the fifth century is available in Pickard-Cambridge, *DFA* and *DTC;* and Bieber, *HGRT* (listed above, "Sources"). Webster in *Greek Theatre Production* (above, "Sources") extends his discussion into greater detail for the later theater of Menander. O. Taplin, *Greek Tragedy in Action,* London, 1978, gives chap. 6, "Objects and Tokens," to properties. The best detailed discussion of any aspect is L. M. Stone, *Costume in Aristophanic Poetry,* New York, 1981.

CHORUS

A selection of the varieties of nondramatic choral song is conveniently presented in translation in R. Lattimore, *Greek Lyric*

Poetry, Chicago, 1960. The same author's translation of the choral songs of Pindar (a near-contemporary of Aeschylus) composed for victors in the athletic games of Greece is also recommended. Evidence on training and preparation is collected in Pickard-Cambridge, *DFA.* Detailed speculations on the choral origins of both tragedy and comedy are to be found in Pickard-Cambridge, *DTC.*

83

ACTORS

Pickard-Cambridge, *DFA,* chap. 3, contains most of the ancient evidence, and a scheme for the distribution of roles between performers. The evidence linking Euaion and Sophocles is discussed by T. B. L. Webster, *Potter and Painter in Classical Athens,* London, 1972; and presented in the introduction, "Theatre Art and Its Patrons," to Trendall and Webster, *IGD* (above, "Sources"). Some conclusions about acting technique can be drawn from Taplin (above, under "Masks . . ."); and McLeish (above, under ". . . Festivals").

THE PLAYING SPACE

The best summary description is in Webster, *Greek Theatre Production* (above, "Sources").

THE AUDIENCE

The most informative study in the relationship between the Athenian audience and its theater is V. Ehrenberg, *The People of Aristophanes,* 2d ed., Oxford, 1951. For tragedy, N. Loraux, *Tragic Ways of Killing a Woman,* Cambridge, Mass., 1987, examines attitudes surrounding women characters in the theater;

as does "The Conception of Women in Athenian Drama," an extended essay by the editor in H. P. Foley (ed.), *Reflections of Women in Antiquity,* New York, 1981. Aspects of social history are conveniently grouped in a publication by the Joint Association of Classical Teachers, *The World of Athens,* Cambridge, 1984. Details and diagrams of the political assembly place are given in Travlos (above, "The Theater") under "Pnyx." The audience and the community feature prominently in the studies collected by J. J. Winckler and F. I. Zeitlin (eds.), *Nothing To Do With Dionysos?: Athenian Drama in Its Social Context,* Princeton, 1990. A technical view of one convention of contact with the audience is advanced by D. Bain, *Actors and Audience: a Study of Asides and Related Conventions in Greek Drama,* Oxford, 1977.

DELIVERY

The best approach to the problem of "delivery" in the Athenian theater is to read speeches from the law courts and political assembly from a comparable period: one available selection is *Greek Political Oratory* in the Penguin Classics series. Highly sophisticated, contemporary speech composition on a theme close to tragedy is represented by Gorgias' *Encomium of Helen,* translated with an introduction by D. M. McDowell, Bristol, 1982. R. G. A. Buxton, *Persuasion in Greek Tragedy: A Study of Peitho,* Cambridge, 1982, is useful in relation to this and the previous topic.

DISTANCE AND PHYSICAL ACTION

The action of tragedy is the subject of Taplin's book (above, "Masks . . ."); and comedy in performance is the subject of the book by McLeish (above, ". . . Festivals"). D. Seale, *Vision and Stagecraft in Sophocles,* London, 1982; and M. Halleran, *Stagecraft in Euripides,* London, 1984, should also be considered.

CHORAL SONG AND CHORAL ACTION

Discussions of the dramatic chorus have usually been confined to language: for example, R. W. B. Burton, *The Chorus in Sophocles' Tragedies,* Oxford, 1980; to which the different approach of C. P. Gardiner, *The Sophoclean Chorus,* Iowa, 1987, can be compared. L. Aylen, *The Greek Theater,* London, 1985, proposes a scheme of interpretation for the tragic chorus. T. B. L. Webster, *The Greek Chorus,* London, 1970, looks closely at the evidence for dance steps and types. Most critical studies of the individual dramatists contain some observations on the "role" of the chorus, with emphasis on an active chorus strongly marked in relation to Aeschylus and Aristophanes. An extended analysis of the complex forms, including the *parabasis,* of Aristophanes' comedies is available in Pickard-Cambridge, *DTC,* in a discussion which contains some suggestions on presentation.

PARODY

All books on Aristophanes will make some reference to parody. An interesting comparison of three different tragic treatments of the same myth (*Philoctetes*) in an order that we can determine (Aeschylus—?, Euripides—431 B.C., and Sophocles—409 B.C.) survives from the Roman imperial period, and is translated in D. A. Russell and M. Winterbottom, *Ancient Literary Criticism,* Oxford, 1972, chap. 12A. B. Knox, *Word and Action: Essays on the Ancient Greek Theatre,* Baltimore, 1979, has a valuable essay in chap. 19, "Euripidean comedy." For parody as it affects women in an important play for the subject, see F. R. Zeitlin, "Travesties of Gender and Genre in Aristophanes' *Thesmophoriazousae*," another essay in the collection edited by Foley (above, "The Audience").

TRANSLATION AND ADAPTATION

One of the best modern (though not now contemporary) reviews of translation is by P. Green, *Essays in Antiquity*, London, 1960, chap. 9, "Some Versions of Aeschylus," which has a commentary on a number of the translations here. Further commentary on the translation by MacNeice (from Michael Sidnell) and the version by Tony Harrison (from R. B. Parker) is available in M. Cropp, E. Fantham, S. E. Scully (eds.), *Greek Tragedy and Its Legacy: Essays Presented to D. J. Conacher*, Calgary, 1986. Major works exist by G. Steiner, on translation (*After Babel: Aspects of Language and Translation History*, London, 1975); and on "versions," or adaptation and influence (*Antigones*, Oxford, 1984). J. R. Mackinnon, *Greek Tragedy into Film*, London, 1986, explores adaptation into one contemporary medium. The literature on translation is extensive, but some acute perceptions are expressed in particular by W. Benjamin, "The Task of the Translator," in *Illuminations*, London, 1970, a volume of his essays edited by H. Arendt. The fragments of Sophocles' *The Searching Satyrs* provided the inspiration for Tony Harrison's playscript *The Trackers of Oxyrhynchus*, London, 1991.

TRANSLATIONS

A complete series of translations of Greek tragedy and of the comedies of Aristophanes is available in Penguin Classics. A second series of translations, *The Complete Greek Tragedies,* is published by the University of Chicago Press, and includes a translation of Euripides' satyr play, *Cyclops.*

Other translations of individual plays, or groups of plays, are also available, and parallel Greek/English texts are published in the Loeb Classical Library (Heinemann), and by Aris and Phillips.

The translated plays and fragments of Menander are available in Penguin Classics.

PLATE 1. Performer and chorus. Antikenmuseum Basel und
Sammlung Ludwig, Inv. BS 415: Attic red-figured column *krater*,
about 480 B.C.: photo Claire Niggli.

PLATE 3. Detail, lower panel: Prometheus and satyrs. Ashmolean Museum, Oxford, 1937.983: Attic red-figured *kalyx krater,* by the Dinos Painter, about 425–420 B.C.

PLATE 2. Side A: Performers dressing (also known as "Actors dressing"). H. L. Pierce Fund, courtesy Museum of Fine Arts, Boston, 98.883: Attic red-figured *pelike,* by the Painter of the Boston Phiale, about 430 B.C.: h. 24.1 cm., diam. 18 cm.

PLATE 4. *Aulos* player flanked by performers dressed as cocks.
Collection of the J. Paul Getty Museum, Malibu, California,
82.AE.83: Attic red-figured *kalyx krater*, unknown artist, after 415
B.C. Terra-cotta: h. 19 cm., diam. 23.2 cm.

PLATE 5. Illustration of Euripides' *Andromeda*. Staatliche Museen zu Berlin, Antikensammlung, V.I.3237: Attic red-figured *kalyx krater*, about 400 B.C.

PLATE 6. Illustration of Euripides' *Antiope*. Antikenmuseum Berlin, Staatliche Museen preussischer Kulturbesitz, F3296: Sicilian red-figured *kalyx krater*, by the Dirce Painter, about 380 B.C.: photo Isolde Luckert.

COMMENTARY ON
THE PLATES

PLATE 1. An Athenian wine-mixing bowl (*krater*) from the period of the Persian Wars, just before the earliest surviving plays. The six singing and dancing figures wear diadems and sleeveless patterned jackets. The similarity of the faces, and the pronounced jaw line, strongly suggest masks. The different positions of the arms may indicate a sweeping gesture of obeisance to the figure wrapped in a cloak, who rises behind a stepped and adorned altar or tomb. The number of the dancers is half that of the early tragic chorus.

PLATE 2. An Athenian jug (*pelike*), from the period of Euripides' *Medea* and *Hippolytus*. Two members of a (tragic) chorus of women, identified as such from the similarity of their masks. The performer on the right has bound his hair, in preparation for putting on his mask, and both wear (soft) boots with curved toes. The second performer is fully costumed and masked, and hands a final garment to the first, with a "theatrical" gesture. The illustration comes from the Phiale Painter, who shows a strong interest in the theater in his works.

PLATE 3. The lower panel of a painting on an Athenian wine-mixing bowl. One of a series of pictures which seem to illustrate a lost satyr play by Aeschylus, composed a generation before, in which Prometheus brought fire to men in fennel stalks, helped or hindered by satyrs. These satyrs bear no traces of theatrical costume, but the gestures and steps are almost certainly those of performers. It is likely that more than one moment of a dance is shown here—aspects of a sequence—which illustrates the problems surrounding the reconstruction of theatrical dance.

PLATE 4. An Athenian wine-mixing bowl from the later fifth century. A rare illustration of comedy from this period, with two performers as fighting cocks, on either side of a pipe player. They are wearing decorated body stockings, and loin-cloths to which the tail and erect *phallos* are fixed, in addition to wings, masks, and spurs. They may be members of a comic chorus, or paired comic performers in conflict. The presence of the pipe player and their movements suggest they are dancing. The chorus of Aristophanes' *Birds* was of wild birds, but the picture provides us with a model.

PLATE 5. An Athenian wine-mixing bowl, from the end of the fifth century. The named figure of Andromeda stands with her arms fastened to rocks, in a decorated sleeved costume, and wearing an oriental headdress, as does Kepheus, her father, to her right. To her other side stands Perseus, her rescuer. Above Kepheus is Hermes, the guiding god, and above Perseus the goddess Aphrodite (not fully shown), holding a wreath over his head. The boxes would contain offerings, and the painter has shown leaves and shrubs, in addition to the rocks. Almost certainly an illustration of Euripides' lost tragedy *Andromeda,* with clear indications of setting: but not all of these figures would have been in front of the audience at the same time, so it might be termed a composite picture. The parody of this play by Aristophanes in *Women at the Thesmophoria* reveals that there was an Echo in the cave behind Andromeda.

PLATE 6. A Sicilian wine-mixing bowl, of about 380 B.C. Again a composite picture, here of Euripides' late tragedy *Antiope*. Lycus and Dirce persecuted Antiope, and her sons took revenge on Dirce by tying her to a bull: her death is pictured on the left, but would have been reported by a messenger. To the right Zethos and Amphion, the sons of Antiope, are shown about to kill Lycus. They are restrained by the god Hermes, who has appeared above on the *mechane*. Antiope runs away on the right. The painting (like plate 5) has clear indications of setting, in the rocks, trees, and the animal skin, and the climax of the play is shown taking place in the mouth of the cave that had been the home of Amphion and Zethos.

GENERAL INDEX

Numbers in boldface type refer to principal
treatments of the subject

Actors and performers, 7, 8, 14, 23,
25–29, 43–48, 53–56, 59, 60–
61, 69; and chorus, 53–56; and
comic costume, 20, 96; and
masks, 17–19; number of, 15, 18,
25–29; playwrights as, 10, 25–
26, 28–29; and singing, 26–29,
57–58, 59; and tragic costume,
19–20, 95

Aeschylus: and his actors, 28–29; as
character in *Frogs,* 37, 59; his
tragedies as an influence on Euripides, 62–63; his use of costume, 19–20; number of his
plays, 5

Akropolis, 2, 10, 11, 48

Altars, 45, 53–54, 95

Aristophanes: his revision of *Clouds,*
35; his use of costume and properties, 20–21; his use of parody,
21, 41–43, 57–62; his use of the
scene building, 32–33; masks in
his comedies, 18, 96; number of
his plays, 5

Assembly, 35, 38, 42, 48; parody of
its formulas in *Women at the Thesmophoria,* 61; on Pnyx hill, 32,
34; speaking platform (*bema*) in,
45

Athenian citizens, 8, 14, 33–35, 37,
57, 62; as *choregoi,* 7; as composers of plays, 2, 10. *See also* Assembly; Audience; Democracy

Athens, 2, 4, 10, 17, 22–23, 32, 34;
immigrants in, 34; narrative
painting in, 15; purchase of texts

in, 59; worship of Dionysus at,
6–7, 17, 22–23

Attica, 7, 60

Audience, 1–2, 7, 11, 29, **33–38,**
52, 54, 69, 70; addressed by
characters or chorus, 24, 26, 28;
and its reactions to performance,
9, 27, 35, 40, 43, 57; the modern, 67, 73; and parody, 60–64

Chants, 54, 56, 70

Choregos/-oi, 7, 8, 25

Chorus, 7, 10, 11, **22–25,** 27, 29,
32, 44, 45; and actors in comedy,
28, 46; and actors in early tragedy, 26, 95; addressed by characters, 26, 31–32, 39–41; comic
costumes for, 20, 96; later decline
of, 60–61; and the *Parabasis,* 24,
56; and physical action, 25, 46,
47–48, 52–56; and the playing
space, 29–31; tragic masks and
costumes for, 17–19, 95. *See also*
Dance; Songs and choral singing;
Verse and meter

Citizens. *See* Athenian citizens

City Dionysia, 18, 28, 34; comedy
and tragedy at, 23–24, 57; competition for actors at, 25–26; organization of, **6–8;** revivals at,
60. *See also* Audience; *Choregos;*
Competitions; Festivals of Dionysus; Lenaea

Competitions, dramatic, 6–7, 10;
for actors, 25–26, 27; judgment
of, 36–37; prizes for actors in,

99

INDEX OF PLAYS

(Ae.) = Aeschylus; (S.) = Sophocles; (E.) = Euripides;
(Ar.) = Aristophanes